ENDORSEM

Our world and our culture need this book more than ever! In a world that seems obsessed with sex and simultaneously confused about sex constantly, it's nice to know that God's nearly 3,000-year-old letter has wisdom that can help with our sex lives. It's so easy to forget that God created sex. It was His idea. In the Garden of Eden, before the Fall, God told Adam and Eve to be fruitful and multiply. That's Hebrew for "bow chicka wow wow." God invented sex and He has a purpose and plan for it for our joy and His glory. Pastor Phil Hopper has broken this all down for us so we can understand what can be complicated and lost in translation. He's a world-class preacher and this book will help you navigate the complexities of relationships, sex, and marriage if you will lean in.

Pastor Joby Martin
Lead Pastor, The Church of Eleven22
Author, *If the Tomb Is Empty, Anything Is Possible*,
and *Run Over by the Grace Train*

If you're married, about to get married, or ever desire to be, Pastor Phil Hopper's *Living Your Love Story* needs to be at the top of your reading list. With his highly accessible writing style, Hopper's fresh take on Song of Solomon speaks with humor and intelligence into a subject our culture so desperately needs.

Matt Carter
Vice President
Send Network

We live in a world that is fascinated with sex—and with good reason. God's design for sex inside of marriage includes more than the miracle of procreation—it ignites passion and excitement, joy, and intimacy! In a world that has maligned, misunderstood, and misrepresented sex, Pastor Phil Hopper reminds readers of its powerful purpose in his newest book, *Living Your Love Story*. Using the Song of Solomon, Phil takes readers on a journey toward understanding and enjoying the gift of sex within the context of marriage. Whether you're married, single, dating, or divorced, this book will encourage you as you navigate a sexually confused culture through the eyes of a disciple of Jesus.

Heidi St. John
Author, Speaker, and Founder of Faith That Speaks

The reality is that we invest more time and research in buying an appliance than in our relationships. Phil Hopper compels us to believe that there is a better way. Whether you are single, married, or single again, *Living Your Love Story* meets you where you are and leads you to the redemptive hope we all need for our own love stories.

Ryan Kwon
Lead Pastor of Resonate Church
Fremont, CA

My friend Phil is a gifted communicator of the Scriptures and a wonderful pastor. The care he took in biblically unpacking what can be a sensitive subject in much of Christianity is evident. I believe he offers us a welcome addition to the volumes written on Song of Solomon, which will greatly help the Church.

Léonce B. Crump Jr.
Founder, Renovation Church
Author, *Renovate* and *The Resilience Factor*

My good friend Phil Hopper's new book, *Living Your Love Story*, is such a gift! We live in a world that on one hand is obsessed with romance, relationship, and sex, but on the other hand is so dysfunctional in approaching them. Phil writes with a scholar's mind and a pastor's heart, as he gives such practical wisdom. I believe this book will save so much heartbreak and bring hope and healing to many.

Bruce Frank
Lead Pastor, Biltmore Church

Phil Hopper is a dear friend and a faithful expositor of God's Word. His unique ability to bring practical everyday advice from the truth found in the text is rare! This devotional from the Song of Solomon is born from the preaching ministry of my brother and is filled with practical insights and wisdom found in this passionate love story from the pages of Scripture. You will be challenged, encouraged, and inspired as you unfold the pages of this book!

Vance Pitman
President, Send Network
Author, *The Stressless Life* and *Unburdened*

Pastor Phil Hopper offers us real-life practical wisdom on dating, romance, marriage, and sex based on the biblical love story found in Solomon's Song of Songs—a book of the Bible too often treated as if it's not in the Bible. You'll profit from Solomon's love song and Phil's practical wisdom.

Dr. Larry Osborne
Pastor and Author
North Coast Church | Owl's Nest

Anything God-given is at its very best when it is God-governed, and this book drives this truth home in a powerful way. The Song of Solomon is an amazing marriage of rich theology and beautiful allegory, and Phil navigates it perfectly. Don't just read it, meditate on it and pray over it as you dive deep into its pages. Phil's knowledge and grasp of the Scriptures, history, and life experience will be a great blessing to anyone who reads it, whether single or married.

J. Mark Johns
Lead Pastor, Canvas Church FL

LIVING
Your LOVE
STORY

DESTINY IMAGE BOOKS BY PHIL HOPPER

The Weapons of Our Warfare:
Using the Full Armor of God to Defeat the Enemy

Defeating the Enemy:
Exposing and Overcoming the Strategies of Satan

Living Your Love Story:
Timeless Wisdom for Dating, Marriage, and Intimacy

LIVING
Your
LOVE
STORY

TIMELESS WISDOM FOR
DATING, MARRIAGE, AND INTIMACY

PHIL HOPPER

DESTINY IMAGE® PUBLISHERS, INC.
P.O. Box 310, Shippensburg, PA 17257-0310
"Publishing cutting-edge prophetic resources to supernaturally empower the body of Christ"

This book and all other Destiny Image and Destiny Image Fiction books are available at Christian bookstores and distributors worldwide.

For more information on foreign distributors, call 717-532-3040.
Reach us on the Internet: www.destinyimage.com.

ISBN 13 TP: 978-0-7684-8352-9
ISBN 13 eBook: 978-0-7684-8353-6

For Worldwide Distribution, Printed in the U.S.A.
1 2 3 4 5 6 7 8 / 29 28 27 26 25

DEDICATION

I dedicate this book to my wife, Christa. I am so
blessed by you. You embody Proverbs 31:10-12,
*"Who can find a virtuous wife? For her worth is far above
rubies. The heart of her husband safely trusts her; so he
will have no lack of gain. She does him good and not evil
all the days of her life."* Thank you for faithfully
Living Your Love Story.

ACKNOWLEDGMENTS

This book would never have been accomplished without the tireless work of my remarkable friend and executive assistant, Lisa Deacy. Lisa, thank you!

And thank you to the beautiful bride of Christ known as Abundant Life. It's my greatest joy and honor to be your pastor. Thank you for living His "Love Story" and being living proof of a loving God to a watching world.

CONTENTS

FOREWORD

I had to dig deep to access my first memories of the Song of Solomon.

Being raised in a Baptist meets Pentecostal meets Presbyterian context, the Bible was central to my adolescence and our family. I memorized verses and Catechisms and stories and characters; and on balance, it all felt pretty normal to me.

But around age 10, I remember stumbling onto this Old Testament book that was really weird and strangely interesting. It seemed like a guy and a girl were writing love notes back and forth to each other. As I was about to start puberty, I remember connecting the dots, as best as a kid could, and discovering that there was a part of the Bible that talked about love and how guys feel about girls. They were also, evidently, noticing each other's bodies and comparing certain parts to things like pomegranates and flocks of sheep. I felt a combination of confusion, arousal, embarrassment, and intrigue. And I hoped that nobody would catch me reading it because it felt sort of PG-13, and I felt a little naughty when I read it.

After three decades of ministry, I think this describes how most Christians see this book of the Bible. Often overlooked or intentionally skipped over, the Song of Songs (as it is also known) is a deep well of allegory, symbolism, and meaning on multiple layers. It dignifies the desire that a husband and wife feel for one another. It elevates sexual intimacy in marriage by exploring the differences, similarities, struggles, and passions that God has hardwired into His good design for spouses.

And most importantly, it acts as a foreshadowing of the coming Messiah who will take for Himself a pure and spotless bride to be His forever in an eternal covenant that will never be broken.

I definitely didn't see any of that the first time I read it. Or the 100th time. Years later in college it would take a teacher to tell me, and that is what Pastor Phil Hopper does here for all of us in *Living Your Love Story*.

With precision and clarity, he peels back the layers and the language of Solomon and his Shulamite lover and translates it for plain folks in understandable language. Phil has done the hard work of study, interpretation, and research so that you and I can make sense of what God is actually saying to us about love and romance and relationships today.

My wife and I have written a few books on dating and marriage ourselves, and I can say with honesty that I've never read a more helpful work on the subject than *Living Your Love Story*. The reason is simple; I read Christian books through the lens of the church member sitting in a seat on Sunday morning. I ask myself if the average churchgoer, who attends twice a month, is struggling to get it all done on a daily basis, and really has a desire to know God and have a healthy marriage, would be able to understand and apply what they read.

That's precisely what makes this book so strong. It's theologically rich, keeping your attention with the depth of understanding needed to unpack a 3,000-year-old love story. At the same time, it's readable, memorable, and doable. You will be able to actually put biblical principles into practice right now in your relationship, engagement, or marriage.

And the bonus? There is terrific content for singles, college students, newlyweds, and seasoned couples as well as those who are single again, dating again, or living without a spouse.

I cannot possibly oversell how helpful and practical this book felt on every page. I was constantly learning new insights and connecting words and meanings that I had totally missed for decades. I know your own relationship with God will be strengthened, not to mention your future or current marriage relationship. I plan to get a copy for both of my sons so I can hand it to them once they are ready to tie the knot.

Dr. Clayton King
Teaching Pastor, Newspring Church and Biltmore Church
Founder of Crossroads Camps, Missions and Conferences
Author, *Reborn, Stronger* and *Overcome*
Anderson, South Carolina

INTRODUCTION

Do you remember the first time you laid eyes on the person you would eventually fall in love with and marry? I do. If you're still single, hang on before you decide this book isn't for you. We are only three sentences in, and I promise much of it is written for singles like you.

But before we go any further, let me share with you the first time I saw the girl I would one day marry. The year was 1985 B.C. (Before Christa). As the summer before my junior year of high school was ending, I got together with some friends. One of my female friends in the group told me about a new girl coming to our high school for the first time. She said she had such beautiful green eyes they couldn't possibly be real. I noted right away the jealous tone as my friend said, "She must be wearing colored contact lenses." I remember thinking to myself, *Wow. This girl must really be amazing.*

I didn't think about it again until the first week of school when I saw the new girl walking down the hallway. I knew instantly that she was the one my friend told me about. I remember thinking she was the most beautiful girl I had ever seen. The only problem—she was holding hands with her boyfriend—one of the cool kids in school who drove one of the hottest cars. To be clear, I was a cool kid, but then there were the *really* cool kids. She was clearly out of my league. What I could not have imagined was that one day I would marry the new girl. Her name was Christa, and those beautiful green eyes were really hers. I was destined to fall in love with those eyes and everything else about her.

That's a little about how our love story began many years ago. And now you are about to hear the love story of a man in history known as King Solomon and his Shulamite bride. The love story he's going to share in the pages of this book is the greatest love story ever told because it's not only a story about his love for his bride but also God's love for us.

King Solomon and the Shulamite

Song of Solomon is about being single and dating, progressing to love, marriage, sex, and romance. It's the story of the Jewish King Solomon and the romance and courtship of his bride. The one known as *the Shulamite* was the love of his life. In the following pages, you will see it's about so much more. It's also about another Bridegroom who loves and romances His bride; a Bridegroom who even died to give life to His bride. I'm talking, of course, about the Lord Jesus Christ.

This Old Testament book—Song of Solomon—doesn't get much attention, preaching, or even reading. You're in good company if you don't know much about Song of Solomon. There are plenty of reasons why.

Many people find Song of Solomon difficult to follow because it wasn't written in our modern English vernacular. It's poetry, but it's not like our modern poetry, which is built on rhythm and rhyme. Ancient Hebrew poetry and songs were built on parallelism, comparison, and contrast. Because you can't read Song of Solomon chronologically, its sudden flash-backs and fast-forwards can be confusing. It can be difficult to follow who's speaking and what's happening.

Another reason Song of Solomon is so difficult to study is that it was written thousands of years ago. Like any culture in history, the Hebrews had their own euphemisms and figures of speech. If you're not part of that culture, time, and place in history, it can go right over your head. This book you're now reading, *Living Your Love Story*, does the hard work of interpreting the remarkable song line by line, revealing the many hidden gems that will make this read well worth your time. This song, composed by Solomon, became a book in the Bible many years ago. So not only are we about to study the lyrics of a song, but a book in the Old Testament.

Anytime you study the Bible, you should begin by asking three questions:

1. What happened historically?
2. What is God teaching?
3. What is the practical application?

Let's look at each question in depth.

First, historically, what happened? The Bible is real history about real people, real events, and real places. All serious study must begin there. Historically, Song of Solomon is a love song—a poem composed by Solomon and put to music to tell the story of his love for his bride and his bride's love for him. His father was King David, and Solomon reigned as king in ancient Israel from approximately 970–931 BC, following his father's death. It's believed he composed this love song sometime early in his reign after meeting and marrying the love of his life–the wife of his youth. Part of it was probably even written and composed to be sung at Solomon's wedding feast.

Next is the doctrinal or theological application: What is God teaching? Theologically, Song of Solomon is an amazing story about the love relationship between Christ and His Gentile bride—you and me—the Church. God wants to teach us not only about our relationship with our spouses in marriage but also about our relationship with Him. That's right. The Bible calls Jesus a Bridegroom, and we, the Church, are called the bride of Christ (Ephesians 5:22-32).

Last, what is the practical application? What does this 3,000-year-old document have to do with my life today? Song of Solomon provides a godly step-by-step guide for navigating relationships with the opposite sex—whether you're single, engaged to be married, or you've been married for decades like me. I wrote *Living Your Love Story* to bring 21st-century clarity to the eternal truths found in this book. It's also a practical manual on how to navigate being single, dating, conflict resolution, sex, and romance. God has given us a beautiful handbook from Heaven on how to date as a single person, how to pursue a mate in a healthy way, how to live happily with your spouse, and how not to let the "honey" disappear from the marriage after the honeymoon is over.

> Satan, sin, and society have all hijacked the discussion around the subject of sex because it is sacred to God.

Now, I must warn you that this book is sure to make some readers blush. Historically, we don't talk about sex in our Christian subculture. Certainly not in the kind of church I was raised in—it makes too many people squirm. But God doesn't get uncomfortable when He hears the word "sex." To Him, sex is sacred. God made it for more than making babies.

I'm convinced that part of the problem in our depraved world is that we have refrained from talking about real-life issues in the Church. We have let the world frame the discussion around sex for far too long. Satan, sin, and society have all hijacked the discussion around the subject of sex because it is sacred to God. Anything God loves, Satan hates. And anything God wants to use for good, Satan wants to use for evil.

Spoiler alert: we will be talking a lot about sex because the very thing God wants to give you in marriage is also the very thing Satan has stolen from so many. For some, it's a source of shame and pain. For others, it's a source of profound disappointment. For still others, it's the source of sin and addiction. Satan has turned sex into a prison for many.

> *The thief does not come except to steal, and to kill, and to destroy. I have come that they may have life, and that they may have it more abundantly* (John 10:10).

Jesus said Satan is a thief. The world has hijacked and redefined sex. Satan has possibly stolen something precious and sacred from you and perhaps even imprisoned you. It's time for us to take it back. This book is about breaking free and taking back something precious. Your birthright as a child of God is an abundant life in the Lord Jesus Christ.

There were times throughout church history when Song of Solomon was banned because it is pretty steamy in places. I refuse to sidestep anything in the Bible because God made it part of His Holy Word for a reason.

Historically Speaking...

Let me set the stage, historically, for what you'll discover in the pages that follow. First, Solomon was a composer. First Kings 4 tells us that Solomon composed more than a thousand songs. His father, King David, wrote most of the Psalms. David was the warrior poet who could sling a stone with one hand and play a really mean harp with the other.

Solomon obviously learned a lot from his father and became an accomplished composer in his own right. His opening remarks speak volumes about what follows. In the very first verse of the very first chapter, Solomon says this is the "song of songs." What does that mean? Scripture says Jesus is King of kings. There are a lot of kings, but Jesus is the greatest King. Jesus is Lord of lords. There are a lot of lords, but Jesus is the greatest Lord. Solomon is saying there are a lot of love songs, but this is the greatest of them all.

Song of Solomon begins much like a conversation you might have going to dinner with a couple for the first time. Eventually, you will ask, "So, how did you meet?" Solomon and his bride are telling us how they met. Just like that couple you're joining for dinner, Solomon recalls the memories of how they met and fell in love. Then his bride says something she recalls regarding those early days in their courtship and budding romance.

This back and forth between Solomon and his bride will take us from the moment they first met through their dating relationship, subsequent engagement, and finally, to their wedding and even their honeymoon. They'll even let us in on their first spat. It's going to be good, so let's get started.

1

IT'S TIME TO DEFINE THE RELATIONSHIP

It was the fall of 1987, and I was living my dream at the University of Kansas on a full-ride football scholarship. I was so excited to begin my college football career, but I soon realized I was totally distracted by another dream. The *dream* with green eyes had come to surprise me. I had driven to her house countless times over the past year, and now she had driven to see me. I was seriously living two dreams. It was during football training camp, and the season hadn't even started when Christa and a couple of my high school teammates knocked on my dorm room door.

I was a freshman football player with plenty to prove on the field. At the first team meeting, the coaching staff made it clear there were to be no girls anywhere near our dorms. They didn't want any distractions for the players, and there would be serious consequences for any violations.

After the first practice, one of the team captains, a senior offensive tackle, stood up and looked over at us freshmen and growled, "When Coach says, 'no girls,' he means no girls! Don't get caught messing up." I thought, *Okay. I got it. No problem.*

That was before Christa showed up after hours with two of my high school friends. I didn't know how they found me, but they did. I was so glad to see them. Well, more specifically, I was really, really glad to see her. I invited them all in with a whisper and quickly shut the door. I didn't know what the consequence would be if my coach found out I had a girl in my room, but at that moment, I didn't care. I was willing to risk it all for love. At this point, Christa and I were in the process of defining our relationship. Over the past year, I'd gone from being invisible, to being her friend, to being in a romantic relationship with her. For me, this moment was worth the risk!

As luck (or providence) would have it, I never got caught. That's what this chapter is about—taking risks and the need to redefine the relationship—but not with the one you might think. The most important relationship you will ever have is your relationship with Jesus, the One who literally risked it all for you.

Four years after I risked it all, we were married in a wedding ceremony that lasted 30 minutes at the most, followed by a reception in the church basement that might have lasted two hours.

By contrast, Jewish weddings lasted a full seven days. Part of the marriage ceremony included putting to song the beautiful melodrama of the couple's courtship, romance, relationship, and marriage. On day four of their wedding feast, they would sing their love song to their audience as if they were in a Broadway theater, sharing how they met and how their love grew. In this song, the gospel was on display from beginning to end.

The Good Shepherd-King

You will see how Solomon is a prophetic foreshadow of Christ—the parallels are striking. Both Solomon and Jesus are called *the son of David*, as both were his descendants. Both are also called a *shepherd* and a *king*. In John 10, Jesus is called the Good

Shepherd. First Peter 5:4 calls Him the Chief Shepherd, and the apostle John in Revelation 19 calls Jesus the King of kings. In Song of Solomon, we will see how Solomon foreshadows Christ's first and second coming. The first time, Jesus came as a shepherd, and the second time as a King. One day soon, Jesus will indeed come for His bride and take her back to His Father's house (John 14:2), just as Solomon also came back for his bride.

Like Solomon, the first time Jesus came as a shepherd to lay down His life for the Father's flocks. The second time, He is coming back as the King, not to suffer, but to conquer. The Song of Solomon is not only the love story of Solomon and his bride but of God's love for us—His Gentile bride. It truly is the greatest love story ever written.

Jesus tells us what it means to be a true King in John 10:11: *"The good shepherd gives His life for the sheep."* Every woman wants to be married to a shepherd king—a leader with authority who leads with humility and lays down his life for her daily—like Jesus, our Bridegroom.

As a shepherd king, Solomon is a magnificent portrait of Jesus, and his Shulamite bride is a beautiful, prophetic picture of the bride of Christ. She is from an unidentified place called Shulem. Many scholars believe it was possibly synonymous with *Shunem,* a reference to someone from the village of Shunem in the territory of Issachar in the northern part of Solomon's kingdom. Solomon's bride is a picture of the Church—the Gentile bride of Christ.

In Luke 21:24, Jesus called the dispensation we are currently living in *"the times of the Gentiles,"* when God temporarily turned His attention away from Israel and the Jews to the salvation of the Gentiles. While there are believing Jews today who are members of the Church, the Church today is largely a Gentile (non-Jewish) bride. But according to what Jesus says in Luke

21:24, we know *"the times of the Gentiles"* are coming to an end, and very soon, the heavenly Bridegroom will return for His Gentile bride. Then He will turn His attention once again to the salvation of the Jews (Revelation 7:1-8).

The Bible tells us that Solomon was the wisest man who ever lived. He also had 300 wives and 700 concubines—two perplexing realities. It is frequently asked, "How can he be an authority on marriage when he was obviously far from being in the will of God?"

Unholy Alliances

That is why it is so important to know the historical context of this love story. It was common practice at that time for a king to seal a political or military alliance by marrying another king's daughter or some other relative. Song of Solomon was written early in Solomon's reign. The Shulamite was his first bride when he was still leaning on God rather than political alliances.

Song of Solomon begins with the Shulamite's flashback to when they first met:

> Let him kiss me with the kisses of his mouth—for your love is better than wine. Because of the fragrance of your good ointments, your name is ointment poured forth; therefore the virgins love you. Draw me away! ...I am dark, but lovely, O daughters of Jerusalem, like the tents of Kedar, like the curtains of Solomon. Do not look upon me, because I am dark, because the sun has tanned me. My mother's sons were angry with me; they made me the keeper of the vineyards, but my own vineyard I have not kept (Song of Solomon 1:2-6).

She is so ashamed of her tan that in verse 6, she tells Solomon, *"Do not look upon me, because I am dark,"* comparing her skin's complexion to the tents of Kedar—the Bedouin tents covered by black goat skins that dot the landscape of Israel to this day.

Beauty is cultural. There was a stigma with a woman having a suntan in this young lady's culture. What one culture says is beautiful, another says is not. What is considered physically attractive in the United States today may be regarded as unattractive in other parts of the world. In all of history, America has one of the only cultures in the world that considers a suntan a thing of beauty. Historically, most cultures consider a fair complexion something desirable, and women diligently protect their skin from the sun.

> In the culture of that time, she committed an unforgivable sin.

There are several clues about the Shulamite's identity from the opening stanza of the Song. We know she came from a wealthy family because they had multiple vineyards. She even had her own vineyard. That alone would have been unique in her day. It was even more unusual that she worked with the men in the vineyards, implying that at some point, she sinned and committed a moral indiscretion. She was ostracized and stigmatized by her family. Her father, who would have been the dominant male figure in her life, isn't mentioned. Only her brothers are mentioned. In the culture of that time, she committed an unforgivable sin. In this deeply honor/shame society, she dishonored and shamed her family.

There is a double meaning when she says, *"But my own vineyard I have not kept."* Throughout this love story, gardens and vineyards are a euphemism for sex. She is humiliated for compromising her sexual chastity. It is important to understand how much it meant in ancient cultures for a woman to lose her virginity to anyone before marriage. It is still important today in the eyes of God. You can see why she doesn't want anyone to even look at her. Her brothers were so angry with her for losing her sexual purity that they made her work outside in the sun. She carries the shame of her sin—stigmatized now by her sun-darkened skin. She knew she had probably forfeited the possibility of any man ever wanting to marry her.

Purity Lost; Purity Restored

Because the ancient Hebrews so deeply valued the bride's sexual purity, the bridegroom would place a white cloth underneath his bride before they consummated their marriage. If there was blood on the cloth, it was proof that she was a virgin. One of the first things the bridegroom would do after the consummation was to present that white cloth with his bride's blood on it to her father, proving he had not consummated their relationship too soon. It also proved the honor and chastity of his new bride. If indeed there was no blood, he had a legal right to divorce her immediately.

The Shulamite bride is a picture of all of us—no one has kept their purity spiritually. The apostle Paul wrote in Romans 3:10, *"There is none righteous, no, not one."* And in Romans 3:23, *"For all have sinned and fall short of the glory of God."* The prophet Isaiah understood our inherent sin nature when he said in Isaiah 53:6, *"All we like sheep have gone astray; we have turned, every one, to his own way...."*

We have all sinned again and again. We have repeatedly "slept" with sin. We have lied. We have cheated. We have stolen. We have had ungodly thoughts. We have spoken filthy words, cursing the very God we claim to serve. It may sound harsh, but we are all spiritual prostitutes devoid of purity in our thoughts and actions. This is why we need the Savior—Jesus Christ!

There was a day when our Shepherd King came before His Father and provided the dowry of His sinless, spotless blood for the price of His bride—the Church. Because we forfeited our purity through sin, He shed His blood in our place on the Cross. As Christians, we are His sinless bride, ratified by a blood covenant with our Bridegroom.

The Shulamite was without hope of marriage and love. No man would ever love or cherish her or make her his wife. That all changed one day when she was toiling in her brothers' vineyard, and a shepherd appeared, tending to his flock. Their eyes met. He looked beyond her skin and her past and said, "I think you are beautiful." He redeemed her from her stain. He redeemed her from her pain. And he redeemed her from her shame. Are you beginning to see why Solomon is a beautiful portrait of our Savior? And she is a remarkable picture of us?

Defining the Relationship

Young people today seem to change the definition of their relationships with the opposite sex every day. It can be difficult to keep up with the ever-changing terms and definitions. As a father of young adults and the pastor of a church with a thriving young adult ministry, I do my best to keep track of the contemporary dating culture—especially the Christian culture.

When I was a teenager navigating the dating scene, if you wanted to ask a girl to be committed to an exclusive relationship, you said, "Will you go with me?" That's a funny question considering the first time I popped the question I was still too young to even have my driver's license. We might have liked each other, but we weren't going anywhere unless it was to talk on the phone. In those days, phones were still attached to the wall. We might have been "going together," but we weren't going any farther than the length of the phone cord. It was so awkward in those days trying to have a romantic conversation on the phone with my mom and dad sitting in the living room just a few feet away!

Now, the truth is that I had no training in dating, and I did a lot of things wrong. By the time I got married, my heart wasn't healthy because of my mistakes, but I was just doing what I had seen others do. I was much too young and immature to be in a romantic relationship.

Today, young people call dating something different. When asked to define their relationships with the opposite sex, they will say, "We're just talking." I sometimes think, *Well, it looks like you're talking a lot and only to each other.* Or they will say, "Oh, we're just going to coffee." To which I think, *Hmmm, that sounds a little like a date.* Then they go from talking to coffee to dating.

You may call it what you want, but there comes a time to define the relationship clearly. Where is this going? Is this going to end in marriage? Are we going to seek a true life-long commitment, or is this relationship going nowhere? Our nature is to love the pursuit but not the commitment.

Since you're reading this book, I want you to know that Jesus is pursuing you. He is a hopeless romantic who loves you so much that He freely gave His life for you. It is vitally important to understand that Scripture teaches if you reject Him again and again, there is a point when Jesus will no longer pursue you.

> *Therefore God also gave them up to uncleanness, in the lusts of their hearts, to dishonor their bodies among themselves, who exchanged the truth of God for the lie, and worshiped and served the creature rather than the Creator, who is blessed forever. Amen. For this reason God gave them up to vile passions. For even their women exchanged the natural use for what is against nature* (Romans 1:24-26).

Jesus is wooing you and pursuing you, but if you continue to resist, there's a point where He will give up the pursuit. Twice in just three verses, we read the words, *"God gave them up...."* If you haven't yet, it's time to define your relationship with Jesus without delay. Do it today.

Christa didn't just happen to be in the neighborhood when she came to see me in Lawrence, Kansas, during my freshman football training camp. We were in the process of defining our relationship. Our story began a year earlier in high school. Providentially, in my senior year of high school, the new girl with the beautiful green eyes was assigned a seat right behind mine in our English class. Suffice it to say, I turned around in my seat most of the year.

After three dates, she put me in the friend zone. I was disappointed, even devastated. I really liked this girl. I grew to love her and refused to give up. I pursued her. I wooed her. I served her. We spent a lot of time together as friends. I asked her to go with me to our senior prom, but she turned me down. (She didn't know she was turning down the future Prom King of 1987!) She asked me to dance at our senior prom, and I turned her down. (I could play that game as well.)

I was sick with strep throat on the day of our high school graduation. I was so sick that I wasn't sure until the last minute if I could even show up to walk across the stage. Remarkably, I found the strength to go to her graduation party. That is how much I had grown to care for her, but I was reaching my limit.

I had a full-ride scholarship to play football at the University of Kansas, and I would soon be leaving town for Lawrence, where there would be plenty of pretty girls on campus. I pursued the girl with the pretty green eyes my entire senior year, but it was time to move on until...the night before I left for football camp.

It was late, and I was busy packing when I heard a knock on the front door. It was Christa! She had come to say goodbye. I walked outside, where we stood and talked in the dark, and that is when it happened. We hugged each other to say goodbye, but we didn't let go. This was not going to be goodbye after all. The next thing I knew, we were kissing. It was mid-August. It wasn't the Fourth of July, but I'm certain to this day that I saw fireworks in the sky.

Had Christa not made her move when she did, we would never have gotten married. I would have moved on, and she would have, too. All these years later, our lives would be radically different and tell a much different story. There would be no Jake, Makay, or Josh—our three children who are now young adults. There wouldn't be the joy of sharing grandchildren together. There would be no memories together and no ministry together. We would have lost touch with each other.

That night on my parents' front lawn would forever define the future. Four years later, she would become my bride, and more than 30 years later, we are still going strong and are even more in love. I had made my move, and I'm so thankful Christa finally made hers.

Jesus has made His move; now it is time to make yours. It is time to define your relationship with Him.

Many today are in danger of losing the opportunity to be a part of the bride of Christ because they have said no to Him over and over. Being a Christian is not like being in a part-time relationship with one foot in and one foot out. It is not like being in a casual dating relationship. Jesus is not looking for a girlfriend; He is looking for a bride who will put the ring of commitment on her finger and say, "I understand the relationship, and I forever surrender my will as a sold-out follower of Jesus Christ."

In Romans 1:24, the apostle Paul writes, *"God gave them up,"* and he repeated it in verse 26. And then in verse 28, he says, *"God gave them over."* He gave them up and gave them over to the decision of their hearts. They decided to reject the one true Lover of their souls for the counterfeit lovers of this world. Doctrinally, biblically, and theologically, the Bible teaches there is a point when even Jesus says, "I am done. Have it your way. The invitation is withdrawn." Today is the day to say, "Jesus, I say 'I do' to You," because Jesus said, "I do" on the Cross for you.

God's Love Story

What is Song of Solomon about? What is Scripture about? What is God's story about? It is His love story of the Son of God hanging on the Cross for you and me. And it ends with a bride and Groom and a wedding by the glassy sea. (Revelation 4:6). It is the greatest love story that has ever been and ever will be told!

2

THE BETROTHAL

Many young men today go to great lengths to plan a romantic proposal, even when the bride-to-be knows it's coming. My oldest son, Jake, asked my wife and me to meet him at a beautiful botanical garden. It brought us great joy when he wanted our help to plan his marriage proposal to the love of his life. He shared with us what he was planning as we strolled along the walking trail, stopping at various locations he had chosen, while Christa and I gave him some feedback and ideas.

It made me wish I could have had a do-over. Christa and I knew we would get married long before I officially proposed. She had gone with me to pick out the ring. One night, after going to a movie, I parked the car in front of my parents' house, pulled the ring out from underneath the seat, and simply said, "Will you marry me?" It was an anti-climactic proposal, to say the least. Christa, darling, I'm sorry it was so lame, but what can I say? Things were different in the '80s. Nobody taught us how to propose, and there was no social media back then to compare and try to one-up your friends. Either way, young men today have *upped* the game.

Regardless of all the planning, nothing can compare to the ancient proposal ceremony of the Jewish bridegroom and bride. The ancient Hebrew wedding had three stages, each a beautiful picture of our relationship with our Bridegroom, the Lord Jesus Christ.

First was the betrothal stage. It began with the Ketubah—the covenant or written agreement between the bridegroom and the bride's father that stated the agreed upon "price" of the bride. We would call it a dowry today, although that practice has virtually disappeared. It also included their vows and the promise of fidelity to each other. The Ketubah was legally binding and guaranteed the bride was a virgin.

Today, we call the betrothal stage the engagement, but it was so much more for this ancient Hebrew couple. They were legally married from the moment they signed the Ketubah. The only difference was they could not consummate the marriage. It was sometimes months or even years before that would take place because of the time it could take for the young man to raise the agreed-upon price for his bride.

> The ancient Hebrew wedding is a beautiful picture of our relationship with our Bridegroom, the Lord Jesus Christ.

After signing the Ketubah, the bridegroom would go away to his father's house to prepare a bridal chamber where they would consummate their marriage—the second stage of the wedding ceremony. The consummation was considered so sacred to the ancient Hebrews that it was part of the seven-day wedding feast and took place on the first day while friends and family waited outside the bridal chamber. Talk about pressure! After the consummation on the first day of the wedding celebration, something different would be done to celebrate the couple's love each day for the next six days. On the fourth day, a song like the Song of Solomon was often performed to celebrate the couple's relationship.

The wedding feast was the third stage of the ancient Hebrew wedding and would generally last seven days. Wedding receptions have come a long way since Christa and I gathered with friends and family for cake and punch in the basement of the church on that special day in October 1991. They have gotten more elaborate and much more expensive. But imagine a wedding reception that goes on for seven days without stopping. Wow! Nothing today can even compare.

The three stages of the ancient wedding can be seen throughout Scripture, including Jesus' first miracle at a wedding in Cana when He turned water into wine. It was at a wedding feast very similar to the one Solomon would have celebrated with his bride over 900 years earlier.

As Christians, we are in the betrothal stage of our marriage to Jesus Christ. He has gone to His Father's house, promising to return. The night before His death, He said the following words as a Jewish Bridegroom. His Jewish disciples, men who had undoubtedly witnessed many Ketubah ceremonies, would have instantly understood the words of their Messiah as that of a Jewish Bridegroom. As a married man, the disciple Peter would have said something very similar to his bride upon completing the betrothal ceremony:

> *In My Father's house are many mansions; if it were not so, I would have told you. I go to prepare a place for you. And if I go and prepare a place for you, I will come again and receive you to Myself; that where I am, there you may be also* (John 14:2-3).

Jesus was speaking the words of a bridegroom to a bride-to-be. The word *mansions* can be translated as "rooms." These were the last words spoken by all Jewish bridegrooms at the Ketubah ceremony. He would look at his bride and announce he was going to his father's house to prepare a room for her, a bridal chamber, promising to return. Jesus ascended back into Heaven to go to His Father's house where He is preparing a bridal chamber for His bride, the Church.

After months or sometimes even years, the Jewish bridegroom would reappear unannounced to carry his bride back to his father's house, where the betrothed would finally be fully wed, and the two would become one. While her bridegroom was away, the Jewish bride was always preparing for the day he would suddenly reappear. Because the Ketubah was legally binding, she was assured that he was coming back.

Today Could Be "The Day"

For this reason, she lived every day like it could be "the day." She kept herself completely chaste. At this point, she would not dare risk even a glance in another man's direction. She wanted all other men to know she was already taken. If she had the means, she would go through various beauty treatments, including soaking in perfumed baths. She wanted to be ready.

You can begin to see then what Paul meant when he wrote in 2 Corinthians 11:1-2:

> *Oh, that you would bear with me in a little folly—and indeed you do bear with me. For I am jealous for you with godly jealousy. For I have betrothed you to one husband, that I may present you as a chaste virgin to Christ.*

To put that Scripture in context, the Corinthians were led away by false teachers. They were prostituting the truth with heresy and false doctrine. Their church was full of sin. As the bride of Christ, we've been betrothed to Jesus. Paul is articulating the heart of God. This is why the apostle James would write in James 4:4-5:

Adulterers and adulteresses! Do you not know that friendship with the world is enmity with God? Whoever therefore wants to be a friend of the world makes himself an enemy of God. Or do you think that the Scripture says in vain, "The Spirit who dwells in us yearns jealously"?

Jesus is not jealous *of* you—He is jealous *for* you.

Sinning is cheating on Jesus, our Bridegroom.

That is how Jesus feels about you every time you choose to sin. Much of American Christianity believes we can flip out the grace card at any time, as if God's grace gives us a license to sin.

What shall we say then? Shall we continue in sin that grace may abound? Certainly not! How shall we who died to sin live any longer in it? (Romans 6:1-2)

The apostle Paul declares with great passion that this is a theological paradox—an impossibility. Because of God's love for us, we should be motivated to pursue lives of holiness and purity. Like that ancient Jewish bride waiting for her bridegroom to reappear, we should keep our hearts solely for Him. To Jesus, it's like turning to another lover when we choose to sin.

What do you suppose I would do if today somebody knocked on the front door of my home, and I answered it to see a handsome man standing there with a bouquet of flowers? What if he said, "Good afternoon, Phil. I want to take your wife out on a date. I promise we're not going to sleep together. We've been flirting with each other, and we're probably just going to hold hands and passionately make out. But don't worry; I promise to bring your wife home by midnight."

What would you expect me to say? "Yeah, sure, no problem. You two have a good time." If that were my response, you would probably think I had lost my mind. But that wouldn't be my response. I'm not jealous *of* my wife, but I am jealous *for* my wife. I don't want to share her with another.

I realize we live in such a depraved culture that "swinging" married couples are becoming more commonplace. That is the immoral thinking of a depraved mind. Normal human thinking is to want our spouse's love and affection for ourselves. I would probably tell that handsome man to call 911 because there is about to be bloodshed—and I don't mean mine. I am about to physically throw him off my porch and threaten his life if he ever comes back again. That is how Jesus feels whenever we choose another lover instead of loving only Him.

When we choose sin instead of Jesus, we are saying His love is not enough and that we need another lover who will really satisfy us. From that perspective, it is easy to see why Paul says Jesus is *jealous over us with a godly jealousy.* He wants our hearts solely for Him. He wants us to keep ourselves solely for Him. As Christians, this is what we are called to do while we wait for our Bridegroom to reappear for His bride.

While We Wait

Just as the ancient bridegroom came unannounced, Jesus will suddenly appear one day and take His bride to His Father's house. We commonly call it the Rapture of the Church, and you can read about it in 1 Thessalonians 4:16-18. What do we do as the betrothed bride of Christ? We keep our hearts solely for Him. We reject sin and all the other lovers that come calling.

If you're harboring sin in your life, now would be the perfect time to confess it and turn from it. It is time for a break-up of the best kind. Sin is not your friend. This world, full of sin, is also full of broken promises. Sin leads only to pain and sorrow.

Right now, before going any further in this book, how about you come back to the Lover of your soul—Jesus, the true

Bridegroom, who will love you and never leave you. In fact, He promises to *"never leave you nor forsake you"* in Hebrews 13:5. He alone knows you intimately, and He loves you perfectly. Despite your faults, flaws, hitches, and hangups, He loves you unconditionally.

If you have given yourself to the false lovers of this world, claim the promise of 1 John 1:9: *"If we confess our sins, He is faithful and just to forgive us our sins and to cleanse us from all unrighteousness."* Pray, "Jesus, I confess my sin. Please forgive me. I'm turning now from my sin and turning to You. Thank You for receiving me and loving me so perfectly."

3

SINGLE, SATISFIED, AND READY

Song of Solomon begins when Solomon and the young maiden are single. As a single Christian, seek your contentment and satisfaction in your relationship with Jesus. If you can't be content as a single person, you won't suddenly become content once you're married. This is why so many married people live in disappointment. They expected a mere mortal to do something only Jesus could do. Contentment is not built on anything but Christ alone because no one will ever love you more than Jesus. The apostle Paul had much to say about this as a single man himself.

> *Are you bound to a wife? Do not seek to be loosed. Are you loosed from a wife? Do not seek a wife* (1 Corinthians 7:27).

The apostle Paul was talking about finding your contentment in Christ whether you are married or single. I know many single people who cannot wait to be married and at least a few married people who wish they were single. Contentment is not about your circumstances and what happens to you. It has to run much deeper to be truly content wherever life takes you.

True contentment can only be found in Christ. I realize as a single adult, you may long to be married, and finding contentment in Christ sounds all but impossible. I'm not suggesting contentment is easy, but as you grow in Christ, you will naturally grow in contentment. I would also suggest that finding true contentment as a single person while still desiring to be married is not mutually exclusive. But to grow in your contentment as a single even while desiring to be married, you must remember the following:

Christ alone has the power to complete you.

About 40 percent of the adult population in the United States is single, and as a pastor, I minister to many of them. I know many singles feel there is something insufficient or even incomplete about them because they are not married.

Remarkably, I've even heard pastors quote Genesis 2:18 at weddings where God says over Adam, *"It is not good that man should be alone; I will make him a helper comparable to him."* See? Poor Adam was lonely and needed a companion to complete him. No! Adam was already created in the image and likeness of God. It doesn't get any more complete than that.

Before Adam sinned, he and God were in perfect fellowship. Talk about companionship! Adam didn't need a helper or a companion to complete him. He needed someone to help him fulfill the commission God gave him: To be *"fruitful and multiply; fill the earth and subdue it"* (Genesis 1:28). Adam was alone. He was a bachelor. As a bachelor, it was going to be impossible for him to be fruitful while remaining alone. So, God created woman—not to complete him but to help him fulfill his commission. When two people get married hoping to complete each other, instead of completing, they end up competing. No one can complete you except the One who created you. Don't put expectations on another mere mortal to do for you what only God can do.

You see, as a born-again child of God, someone who has received by faith the Son of God, you now bear the image of God. You are as whole a person as you will ever be. If you feel you need somebody else to complete you, let me redirect how you see and think about yourself. Let me encourage you to believe what God says about you regardless of what anyone else says about you.

You + Jesus + Nobody = A Whole Person

I understand why sometimes you might wish you had a real-life flesh and blood person to be married to. I know that single women especially hate the cliché usually repeated by married people, "Remember, Jesus is your husband." (You're probably thinking, *Yeah, well, Jesus doesn't take the trash out in the morning— and a lot of other things I wish I had a husband for.*)

This is what I know: Jesus alone is sufficient for every human need, whether you are married or single. Before Adam walked with Eve, he walked with God, and because he did, God made Eve for him.

God's Pattern for You

A lack of contentment leads to a lack of conviction, and a lack of conviction leads to compromise in our lives. Sometimes, we are willing to settle for less than God's best. We compromise the best God has for us because we get impatient, think God is holding out on us, or somehow, that God is not enough.

When we lack faith in God's Word and character, we are no longer content in our relationship with the Son of God and the Word of God. When that happens, we start compromising in little places and suddenly realize we've lowered our standards and are dating people who aren't marriage material. While this is true for some Christian singles, others are still single because they suffer from "paralysis by analysis."

In fact, I have noticed a pattern, especially within the Christian purity culture of dating, that is quite frankly dysfunctional. It is an overreaction to the cultural method of dating, which is just for fun or a hook-up. Whatever the reason, it shouldn't be as complex as it appears.

A Christian young man asks a Christian young lady on a date, and she says, "No" because he doesn't seem to check all the boxes quite right, or because she hasn't had enough time to observe his character or a myriad of other excuses. Wait a minute. He didn't ask her to marry him. He just asked her to get tacos with him. Stop over-spiritualizing.

If you're single, you may need to go on a date to see if you should go on another date. I'm not talking about random or casual dating, dating without intention, or dating without marriage being the clear destination. But if you never give anyone a chance to get to know you, you will never get to know them. And you will never know what you don't know.

The only way you will get to know the person is to go somewhere and spend time with them. (In my day, it was called a "date," but you can call it "coffee.") After going out that first time, ask yourself a couple of diagnostic questions.

First, are you attracted to the person physically? This matters in marriage regardless of what the purity culture says. Most of the people who say physical attraction doesn't matter are the ones who are already married to an attractive spouse. You are the only one who can say if you think someone is attractive because, as the old saying goes, "Beauty is in the eye of the beholder."

Remember, what is considered physically attractive or beautiful can vary immensely from person to person. This is not about what your friends think. This is about what you think. He or she certainly shouldn't have to be a fitness model to check this box. Don't wait for the perfect "10." But you know whether or not you are physically attracted to them. If you are not, politely decline a second date.

Second, ask yourself if you find them inwardly attractive. Do you enjoy talking with them? Do you sense any attractive inward qualities like humility, integrity, strength, and virtue? Do they share your passionate pursuit of Jesus? Do they desire to grow spiritually and be used by God in meaningful, eternal ways? The answer to the first question is important. But the answer to the second question is vital! It is non-negotiable. In Second Corinthians 6:14, the apostle Paul gives us timeless wisdom on not being "unequally yoked" to an unbeliever. I would suggest the same principle is true for someone who claims faith in Christ, but their lifestyle says otherwise. Or they are just passive spiritually with worldly priorities.

> Marital compatibility has far more to do with a shared spiritual vision and worldview than personalities.

Discussions about marital compatibility tend to focus far too much on personality. Marital compatibility has far more to do with a shared spiritual vision and worldview than personalities. A spiritually shared DNA is more important to marital compatibility than shared interests and hobbies. If you check "yes" to both questions, you should consider going on a second date.

If at any point you decide you are spiritually incompatible, or you just don't connect or share the same vision for the future—you should break off seeing each other and go your separate ways. Immediately. You should not keep hanging around each other as "just friends."

You fall in love with the people you hang around. You might say, "Well, I would never fall in love with that guy." Just hang around him enough, and you might. You may think you can fix him where others have failed. No, you won't. If Jesus hasn't fixed him, you aren't going to fix him. His best behavior is being displayed now before you marry him. That's why it is important to decide ahead of time the profile of the person you want to marry.

Please understand that the most important thing you can do right now is to find your contentment in Christ. Without finding your contentment in Christ, you will compromise and lower your standard of the person you want to marry. When you do, you'll get in a hurry and settle for less than God's best.

As a single person, you may think you are the loneliest person in the world, but that moniker belongs to somebody who is married—only to find they are still lonely. You may think you are lonely by yourself, but you have never been so lonely as when you are lying in a king-size bed with your spouse and realize you are still alone. Sadly, I know people in that situation.

Jesus Is Enough

It is Christianity 101 for the single person to decide that Jesus is enough. Many Christian singles act like being single is a curse, but Paul considered it a gift and thought it better to be single and celibate.

> But I want you to be without care. He who is unmarried cares for the things of the Lord—how he may please the Lord. But he who is married cares about the things of the world—how he may please his wife. There is a difference between a wife and a virgin. The unmarried woman cares about the things of the Lord, that she may be holy both in body and in spirit. But she who is married cares about the things of the world— how she may please her husband. And this I say for your own

profit, not that I may put a leash on you, but for what is proper, and that you may serve the Lord without distraction (1 Corinthians 7:32-35).

Paul is saying to celebrate your singleness. While single, you can use all of your energy, ability, and every opportunity solely for God's glory without the demands of a family.

Use your singleness instead of trying to lose your singleness.

Some who may read this book, perhaps you, have prayed and realized you have the gift of singleness. You do not really care if you get married; you are content by yourself. Others have surrendered everything to Jesus, yet deep down they are still not content. You may have the gift of singleness; you just don't know it yet—or maybe Jesus will bring the right person into your life at the right time. Focus on becoming the kind of person that the person you are looking for is looking for. Focus on *becoming* "the one" instead of always trying to find "the one."

So, what do you do? You follow Solomon and his Shulamite bride's example. While you are single, it is an opportunity to grow in godly character qualities. Real beauty is not simply what you see outwardly. It is rooted in the qualities of fidelity, integrity, purity, and serving others selflessly.

Desirable Qualities in the Man You Marry

In Song of Solomon 1:3, the Shulamite thinks about the man she married: "*Because of the fragrance of your good ointments, your name is ointment poured forth; therefore, the virgins love you.*"

This man is not only handsome outwardly, but he is also handsome inwardly. He has a godly reputation. His very reputation is like a sweet aroma. That should be at the top of the list when deciding about the kind of person you want to marry. That is why the Shulamite says even *"the virgins love you."* This kind of man should be the model for every woman with marriage in mind.

Solomon is the kind of man he is because of his godly virtue. She is attracted to him physically, but the first thing she says about him has nothing to do with his appearance and everything to do with his character. This man has a good name. When he walked into a room, he left a fragrance. This man's very name was like *"ointment poured forth."* He left an aroma of "life" everywhere he went. There are some men who carry with them the aroma of "death." They have a reputation for anger, or bitterness, or sexism, or selfishness. You get the point.

Desirable Qualities in the Woman You Marry

The Shulamite worked outside like a man in the vineyards. Then, one day, she saw this shepherd coming who was obviously very wealthy. He had a great number of sheep and a large entourage. She probably didn't even know she was looking at King Solomon. She was from many miles north of Jerusalem, where King Solomon reigned. She undoubtedly heard of him but had no idea what he looked like. She simply saw a handsome shepherd.

In the last stanza of this song, we find out where and how they met. Spoiler alert! Solomon most likely traveled to the northern region of his kingdom to survey the condition of his personal vineyards. We don't know for sure, but he was likely unrecognizable to the young lady he met working in the vineyards. We do know that the first time they met he merely came as a shepherd. A very handsome shepherd. It was almost love at first sight. There was an immediate and strong attraction between them. As he prepared to leave, she said…

Tell me, O you whom I love, where you feed your flock, where you make it rest at noon. For why should I be as one who veils herself by the flocks of your companions? (Song of Solomon 1:7)

The shepherds were nomadic and followed their sheep, and historically, the prostitutes followed the shepherds. She said, "Do not expect me to throw myself at you because I'm not going to. Do not think I am like the prostitutes who veil themselves and hang around the shepherds' tents after hours." She made a mistake in her past, and she's not about to make that mistake again. This woman's most attractive quality is her virtue and humility. It's what every man wants in a wife. Proverbs 31:10, *"Who can find a virtuous wife? For her worth is far above rubies."* A mystery king named Lemuel is attributed as the author of Proverbs 31, though many biblical scholars believe that was a "pet name" given to Solomon by his wife and that it was written by Solomon as a tribute to his Shulamite bride, the love of his life.

She said, *"Where do you tend your flock at noon?"* In other words, "I am not coming after hours. I am not pursuing you in the dark like I'm a prostitute. Where can I find you at noon because I'm not coming to see you at night." Notice she was practicing virtue while still single. Men and women listen carefully: Virtue and integrity are not character qualities that suddenly materialize in your life once you're married. The truth is, if you aren't living with sexual integrity and virtue as a single person, you're not suddenly going to start once you're married. I'm convinced that part of the problem with this epidemic of marital infidelity in our generation is that people who were used to "sleeping around" and "playing the field" as a single don't suddenly stop just because they put a ring on their finger. You are establishing thought patterns and behavioral patterns while single that will follow you into marriage. This is the age of routine porn use and "body counts." If that's you as a single, I'm trying to lovingly warn you—you are allowing Satan to hijack your marriage ahead of time.

The Shulamite had become not only virtuous but wise. The problem with trying to catch a man with sex is it just might work. If you catch him with sex alone, there's a good chance somebody else will as well. This young woman told Solomon that she was not about to do that. "Don't make me guess where you will be at noon because you won't see me after hours."

They both had a godly virtue. They established that they were people of fidelity, integrity, and godly character. That's the nature of real beauty. As just discussed, it's common to minimize physical looks in the Christian dating culture. "Well, it is all about godly virtue and just marrying somebody with godly qualities and a great personality." It is disingenuous to say physical appearance isn't important. What is also true is how our fallen world places far too much importance on it.

Many people who have been married for more than 50 years find a great deal of things get better the longer they are together. Plenty of things also get worse or eventually change and are never the same. I like what one person said, and it is true for men everywhere: "There is a day coming when you step out of the shower and realize you have 'furniture disease.' Your chest is falling into your drawers."

If you're married, continue to take care of yourself outwardly. Your spouse will be glad you did, and you will be happier and healthier because you do. But outward beauty and physique are fleeting. There better be something more than skin deep, no matter how beautiful or handsome the skin might be.

You can already see that our lovebirds are not only attracted to each other for what they represent and the godly qualities they possess, but they are equally infatuated with each other physically.

I have compared you, my love, to my filly among Pharaoh's chariots. Your cheeks are lovely with ornaments, your neck with chains of gold (Song of Solomon 1:9-10).

Wait! Did Solomon just call her a horse? How could this possibly be seen as complimentary to a young lady? In their day, stallions always pulled chariots, not the mares. One of the military strategies of warfare to overcome an army with chariots was to set fillies loose on the battlefield when they were in heat to create distraction and diversion. Solomon says, "You are so beautiful; I cannot focus on anything else when you are around. He is so enamored that he promises to shower her with jewelry.

While the king is at his table, my spikenard sends forth its fragrance. A bundle of myrrh is my beloved to me, that lies all night between my breasts. My beloved is to me a cluster of henna blooms in the vineyards of En Gedi (Song of Solomon 1:12-14).

The Shulamite was so captivated with Solomon that he invaded her dreams. Their physical attraction was all well and good, but in a successful marriage, you also need to plan for the future and how you will provide for your family.

As a Single Person, How Are You Preparing Yourself for Marriage?

I talked to every young man who wanted to take my teenage daughter on a date. I began by asking him three questions, starting with, "When did you become a Christian?" My daughter, Makay, was very selective, and there weren't many dates before she met and married my son-in-law, Daniel. If he didn't have a good answer to this first question, he would never have gotten past her to begin with.

Next, I asked him to tell me everything he knew about the book of Zechariah in the Old Testament. (I was joking about this one, but the reaction was always priceless!) My last question was how he was preparing for his financial future. I wanted to know if he was godly and could take care of his family. You are not ready to get married if you haven't thought that far ahead.

If you're single, have you considered the kind of person you want to marry? Whatever else a person has going for them, a heart of humility is essential. Without a heart of humility, no one has any business getting married. People without humble hearts always have hard heads, and hardheaded people will never be happily married. Humility is essential to marital happiness.

Humility is a quality Solomon recognizes in his bride-to-be in chapter 1, verse 15: *"Behold, you are fair, my love! Behold, you are fair! You have dove's eyes."* The eyes are the window to the soul. When he says, "You have dove's eyes," he is not necessarily talking about her appearance. A dove is a very gentle creature. He says, "As I look into your eyes, I see a gentle and humble spirit." It is the number one prerequisite to marriage.

If you must always be right and have your own way, do not get married. It will be warfare from the moment you say, "I do."

On the other hand, if you have a heart of humility, you're willing to defer to another, and don't always need to be right—you may be ready to find someone with an equally humble spirit. It was important enough for Solomon to offer this caveat:

It is better to dwell in a corner of a housetop, than in a house shared with a contentious woman (Proverbs 25:24).

The question is, "Are you becoming like Solomon and the Shulamite?" Before they ever found each other, they pursued godly virtues and godly character qualities. They were becoming the kind of people personally they were looking for in another. Yes, they took care of themselves outwardly. They were two very handsome people who were wildly attracted to each other physically. And Solomon certainly had the material capacity to take care of his bride. But even more important, they had a heart of humility toward one another. Throughout this love song, he not only calls her a dove, but she also calls him "my dove" as well—gentle dove-like spirits who would gladly serve each other.

—4—

PATIENT AND PASSIONATE

God wants us to learn about what we *can't* see by His teaching through what we *can* see. He wants us to understand that the marriage relationship between a man and a woman is a picture of the relationship between Christ and His bride, the Church, according to Ephesians 5:22-33.

Marriage and the ensuing sexual relationship are sacred to God because of how He created the first man and woman. Genesis 2:24 records the very first wedding: *"Therefore a man shall leave his father and mother and be joined to his wife, and they shall become one flesh."*

When God brought Adam and Eve together, it was a match made in Heaven. In the sexual union of marriage, you literally join your lives and become one with each other. That one verse expresses God's original purpose in marriage—to seal a permanent relationship between a husband and wife. Marriage was intended to be an unbreakable, lifelong union. Termination of marriage by divorce was not even a concept to consider before sin came into the world.

In Ephesians 5:31, Paul quotes Genesis 2, saying, "The two shall become one flesh," talking about husbands and wives. And then he says, "This is a great mystery, but I speak concerning Christ and the church." He says there is something going on behind the scenes that you can't see. It is a picture of Christ and His bride.

This is why, in the mind of God, the Maker and Creator of marriage, marriage can only exist between a man and a woman. Jesus made this clear in Matthew 19:4. The reason is because of the symbolism God intends in the marriage relationship. Jesus is not a Bridegroom married to another bridegroom. He is married to a bride. And sexual unity in marriage is a picture of our spiritual unity as His bride. Jesus is in us, and we are in Him. These two phrases are found throughout the New Testament that we are "in Him," and He is "in us."

In Song of Solomon chapter 2, the relationship between Solomon and his Shulamite bride is heating up. They are in their courtship stage. In verse 1, the young lady says, *"I am the rose of Sharon, and the lily of the valleys."* In the next verse, Solomon responds, *"Like a lily among thorns, so is my love among the daughters."* What follows is the young woman's fantasy about making love to the one she loves in Song of Solomon 2:3-7:

> *Like an apple tree among the trees of the woods, so is my beloved among the sons. I sat down in his shade with great delight, and his fruit was sweet to my taste. He brought me to the banqueting house, and his banner over me was love. Sustain me with cakes of raisins, refresh me with apples, for I am lovesick. His left hand is under my head, and his right hand embraces me. I charge you, O daughters of Jerusalem, by the gazelles or by the does of the field, do not stir up nor awaken love until it pleases.*

God created us with that desire, and it is perfectly okay when you are in love to want to make love to the one you love. As part of my premarital counseling sessions, I will periodically ask the couple how they are doing, regardless of their age. Is your relationship pure and honorable before God? Are you struggling with sexual temptation or passion? Occasionally, someone will say, "Oh, we do not have any problem with that." My response usually surprises them: "In that case, you should reconsider whether or not the two of you should be getting married." Either they're not being honest with me, or they're not being honest with themselves.

Pure and Honorable

Sexual intimacy is the natural progression when two people are attracted to and in love with each other. There is nothing sinful or shameful about wanting to be with the one you love, but there is wisdom in waiting for marriage to act on those desires. Even when two people love each other, sexual activity outside of marriage is still a sin in God's eyes because it is sacred and not trivial (Hebrews 13:4).

Our obedience toward God always brings the blessing of God.

This is exactly what is happening with this lovesick bride. She is head over heels in love with Solomon and cannot wait to be with him. In verse 5, she says, *"Sustain me with cakes of raisins, refresh me with apples, for I am lovesick."*

In her day, raisin cakes were considered an aphrodisiac. It was an ancient form of Viagra. She tells Solomon, "I want your raisin cakes, big boy." Canaanites believed the seeds increased libido and fertility. They were used in their fertility rites and placed under the bed of the one they loved. This woman is lovesick. It is not a sin to feel this way about the one she loves, but they are not yet married. She is overcome with passion for the man she loves.

In verse 7, she charges the daughters of Jerusalem, *"Do not stir up nor awaken love until it pleases."* She is saying that she loves him and wants to be with him, but that it's not good for them to stir up this kind of love yet. They need to keep it asleep because once it is awakened, it is difficult to put it back to sleep. They want to do this the right way. They want to be godly and walk in sexual integrity and purity. In the end, as badly as she wants Solomon, they choose patience over passion as a betrothed couple.

This is true for every person in every place for all time. God loves each of us infinitely and passionately. As our heavenly Father, He knows us intimately. He wants us to live a life that is truly healthy and happy. That is why God is emphatic in Scripture that sex is for one place and time.

> *Marriage is honorable among all, and the bed undefiled; but fornicators and adulterers God will judge* (Hebrews 13:4).

God is teaching that the marriage bed is undefiled. There is nothing dirty about sex. It is God's gift of pleasure, beauty, intimacy, and great joy within the marriage relationship.

The Pharisees came to Jesus and asked Him if it was lawful for a man to divorce his wife for any reason—like it is today with no-fault divorce. Jesus responded by quoting Genesis 2:

> *Have you not read that He who made them at the beginning "made them male and female," and said, "For this reason a man shall leave his father and mother and be joined to his wife, and the two shall become one flesh"? So then, they are no longer two but one flesh. Therefore what God has joined together, let not man separate* (Matthew 19:4-6).

The Pharisees countered in an attempt to corner Him in verse 7: *"Why then did Moses command to give a certificate of divorce...?"* They were sure they had Him. But Jesus shut them down in verse 8 saying, *"Moses, because of the hardness of your hearts, permitted you to divorce your wives, but from the beginning it was not so."*

In this passage of Scripture, Jesus did not define marriage based on culture but rather creation. God teaches that any sex outside of marriage between a man and a woman is a sin. Marriage, as God intended, is beautiful and meant to bring joy and intimacy.

Animosity and Hostility

Many people think divorce is always a sin. The implication is that divorce itself is not always a sin, but sin is always the cause of divorce. God's ideal is that there would never be divorce because divorce brings about animosity and hostility. There's never such a thing as a clean break; it brings brokenness to a family and distorts the picture God paints through marriage.

God promised in Hebrews 13:5 to *"never leave you nor forsake you."* Jesus is the Bridegroom in a covenant relationship with His bride. Divorce distorts and shatters the picture of God's covenant of love that He has made with everyone who trusts and believes in Him. He says, *"And I say to you, whoever divorces his wife except for sexual immorality, and marries another, commits adultery; and whoever marries her who is divorced commits adultery"* (Matthew 19:9). The Bible is clear that there is such a thing as a biblical divorce, as well as an unbiblical divorce, like most divorces in America today.

Marriage is both sacred and secular. Just because the state says you are divorced doesn't necessarily mean you are divorced in the eyes of God. There's a marriage covenant in Heaven between two Christian people. Jesus said the marriage covenant can be broken through sexual immorality, adultery, and infidelity.

While debated among those who believe and study Scripture, I personally believe that abuse or abandonment are additional reasons for a biblical divorce from Paul's theological dissertation on marriage in 1 Corinthians 7. But one of the clear reasons God allows divorce is sexual sin. If you have an unfaithful spouse who is unrepentant, you are released from that covenant.

Just because you can divorce does not automatically mean you should.

God's heart is always for reconciliation and redemption—to redeem what is lost. If given the opportunity, repentance has the power to restore what has been lost.

God commands that sex is only to take place within marriage because it goes much deeper than merely the physical act. It touches our very soul. Tragically, we have allowed our society to redefine it for us. God created sex. If you do not pursue it in a godly way, you will end up in captivity and slavery.

Solomon and the Shulamite pursue this part of their relationship in the right way. The apostle Paul emphasized and "amened" God's heart on this subject in 1 Corinthians 6:18:

> *Flee sexual immorality. Every sin that a man does is outside the body, but he who commits sexual immorality sins against his own body.*

Every other sin we commit is against God, but Paul clearly distinguished sexual sin from all other sin because sexual sin is against one's own body. Paul could not have fathomed what that meant when he penned those words by the inspiration of the Holy Spirit nearly 2,000 years ago.

Medical science didn't know then what it knows now—that sexual sin alters the brain. God made your brain so it would react a certain way during sexual activity. A chemical in your brain called oxytocin acts as a bonding agent. Women have ten times the amount of oxytocin in their bodies than men. The only time oxytocin levels in men reach the level of women is during and right after sexual activity.

Sex is more than the bonding of two bodies.
It's the bonding of two souls.

Incidentally, oxytocin reaches its highest level in women right after childbirth. It is a bonding agent that helps the mother quickly bond with her child. God intended the sexual union to be a bonding agent between a man and a woman deep in their very souls.

Sexual dysfunction in marriage can often be related to sexual disobedience while dating. If you have a promiscuous lifestyle, sleeping around with one person after another, you tell your brain to bond in multiple places. The more places you have bonded, the more difficult it is to bond intimately with the person you marry. This is why pornography is so destructive. It is not just adult entertainment. You don't understand what you are doing to your brain.

Sexual stimulation causes the brain to release endorphins. It has been clinically proven that pornography can be as chemically addictive as cocaine. You are teaching your brain to bond with images that are not reality. It is a counterfeit. There is an epidemic in America of young adult men who should be at the prime of their sexual energy and yet they need prescription drugs to have a sexual relationship with a real woman. They have looked at so many different images that their brains and bodies no longer function correctly in a real relationship as God intended.

Disobedience breeds dysfunction.

> *Do not be deceived, God is not mocked; for whatever a man sows, that he will also reap* (Galatians 6:7).

When you sow the seeds of sin, you will eventually reap disappointment and even destruction.

While single, as a prodigal son of God, I stepped outside of God's lines in more ways than one. At the time, I didn't realize that I didn't have the spiritual maturity—let alone the emotional maturity to understand the impact. I know I brought dysfunction into my marriage from the day I said, "I do." I have been married for more than three decades now; but in the early days, it wasn't always the marital bliss that people thought. A lot of our exasperation and frustrations were caused by my disobedience toward God while I was single. Sin always makes for an unhealthy heart. And what I didn't know the day I got married was that my own heart wasn't fully healthy.

> *Keep your heart with all diligence, for out of it spring the issues of life* (Proverbs 4:23).

If a spring of water is poisoned below the surface, it is poisoned above the surface. My heart wasn't healthy when I got married because I didn't guard it before I got married. It was soiled by sin. God can purify the waters of the soul but only by confessing and turning from sin.

Abundant Life, Abundant Marriage

God wants you to know what it means when Jesus says in John 10:10, "*I have come that they may have life, and that they may have it more abundantly.*" God created sex for more than just physical gratification and reproduction. He created sex so you can connect on a soul level with another human being. The lie of our society in this hook-up world we live in is that it's "just" sex. Yet, it is not just something you can do and walk away. There is no such thing as casual sex.

The Bible teaches, and science has proven, that you attach part of yourself to every person you have ever been with and every sexual image you have ever seen or fantasized about. Now, if you're wondering if there is any hope for you because you have lived a promiscuous lifestyle like so many others, I want you to know *there is hope.* God is the God of hope and redemption. Through repentance of sin, God can renew your mind.

> *And do not be conformed to this world, but be transformed by the renewing of your mind…* (Romans 12:2).

We've all heard the saying that time heals all wounds. Depending on how much and how long you've lived in sexual sin, this renewal can take a lot of time. This is not a one-and-done, quick-fix kind of thing. In Christ, God promises to make you a new creation where *"…old things have passed away…all things have become new"* (2 Corinthians 5:17). Renewing your mind is a conscious decision to think God's way. His Word reflects both His heart and His mind. The world tells you to think one way. God tells you to think another way.

God intended your sex life to be how you bond deeply with another on the innermost level of your being. This is how God made your brain work from the opening pages of the Bible and the very dawn of humanity:

> *Therefore a man shall leave his father and mother and be joined to his wife, and they shall become one flesh* (Genesis 2:24).

To be joined in Hebrew means "to glue or bond together." It is the reason there is never a truly clean separation or break-up—especially once two people have been sexually intimate. The *glue* of your relationship is the oxytocin that you release every time you come together as a couple in sexual intimacy and intercourse. You can see why a promiscuous lifestyle, extra-marital sex, or pornography is so destructive to a genuinely healthy, satisfying sexual relationship in marriage. Wherever there is sin, something is dead or dying.

The wages of sin is death... (Romans 6:23).

If you choose to live a holy life, you will discover what it means to live abundantly, and you will be both whole and healthy. But if you try to live a whole and healthy life apart from being holy, you will never be fully whole or healthy.

Satan has hijacked sex.

Ultimately, you will choose whom you believe. Will you believe God? Or will you believe the lies of your adversary and your flesh? Our society is where it is because we have believed one lie after another—the lies that say it doesn't matter with whom you have sex, how you have sex, or even when you have sex.

Somebody told me, "I'm sleeping with my husband-to-be. We're not married yet, but I'm not sleeping around. What's the big deal? I'm going to have a monogamous sexual relationship with him."

Here's the big deal: If the two of you are not learning to "die to self" to live in obedience to God before you're married, you won't suddenly begin doing it once you are married. Now is the time to crucify your flesh and establish that pattern in your life every time you are tempted with sin.

Again and again in Song of Solomon, fruit is the symbol of sex. In chapter 2, verse 3, the Shulamite bride-to-be says, *"Like an apple tree among the trees of the woods, so is my beloved among the* sons. *I sat down in his shade with great delight, and his fruit was sweet to my taste.*"

I love peaches and have peach trees at my home. Nothing is better than a peach at the perfect time when it is so ripe the juice runs down your chin. Sometimes, I have been in too much of a hurry to taste it. I can pick a peach at almost the right time, and it will still taste good. It is still sweet, but not as sweet as it would have been if I had waited.

It is the same with sex. You may not be sleeping around with a lot of different people. You may be sleeping with the one you are engaged to marry, but you are picking that fruit too soon. Is it going to be sweet? Of course it is; sex tastes good—but will it taste *as* good? Would it be as sweet if you had waited and not awakened love before its time? You must choose. Do you want to settle for less, or do you want God's best for your life? Too many settle for mediocrity instead of God's best and what He wants for them. I want everything in life that God wants to give me—and so should you.

> God has a plan for your life, and so does Satan.

Everything God wants to give you, Satan wants to steal from you.

God has a plan for your life, and so does Satan. He wants to steal, kill, and destroy everything God wants to give you. Many have let him take away what was meant to bring us the greatest joy, intimacy, gratification, and satisfaction we could ever imagine—all because we chose to pick that precious fruit too soon.

What does that mean for your marriage? When you make that choice too soon, you have "flipped the switch" on what should be the most climactic moment of your life. You have decided that you want an anti-climactic wedding and honeymoon.

The Choice

Because I was still in college, Christa and I planned our wedding and honeymoon on a weekend so I wouldn't miss more than one day of school. Christa graduated in four years and was already working when we got married, while I had been busy cramming four years of college into four and a half years and wouldn't graduate until December. (Can you sense my sarcasm?)

It was a beautiful October day when we took our vows at the church I attended while growing up in south Kansas City. It was approximately 150 miles from the church to our honeymoon destination—a resort on the Lake of the Ozarks in central Missouri. I made that trip in about 25 minutes. (Okay, slight exaggeration.) There was a climactic moment on the horizon of our relationship, and I could not wait to get there. Neither Christa nor I had been living godly lives when we first met and started dating. But Jesus got our hearts in time to save our first night together as a married couple. And I couldn't get to the honeymoon suite fast enough!

That's how God intended it to be when you leave the fruit on the vine until the moment He meant it to be picked—at the sweetest moment it can possibly be. Both Christa and I aligned our lives with Jesus at the age of 21. We vowed before God and each other to have a relationship of virtue and honor before the Lord. I'm not going to lie and say it was easy. We wouldn't get married for another two and a half years.

But my life is living proof that even if you've lived in disobedience, it's not too late to start over and agree with God. Far too many have believed our lying culture. Satan's lies have won again and again through the ages. The mindset of much of today's society is, "This is the 21st century. We are an enlightened society. We are so much better off now that we have thrown away those outdated biblical ideals and morality." But the soaring rates of suicide, STDs, depression, and anxiety tell a different tale. They reveal the reality and consequences of a society in rebellion against God.

We have a wood-burning fireplace in my favorite room in our home, and I'm writing before a delightfully warm and cozy fire. The beautiful thing about a fire is the way it draws people together. It has the power to warm things up, but if that fire ever leaves the area where it's contained, it can destroy everything. That is exactly the toll that sexual sin has taken on countless lives. What God intended to enhance your life to make it more beautiful and intimate than you could ever imagine has also torched countless relationships.

We have become a society where many people are like zombies during an apocalypse. We are walking dead people. The wages of sin is death, and you are dead on your feet if you're living in sin—especially sexual sin—because it brings death and destruction. You may already know that because you have watched it bring death to your marriage, kids, relationships, family, and finances.

You can never sin and win.

You may think you're doing pretty good while living in sin, but a payday is coming someday. God loves you enough to warn you.

> *Whoever commits adultery with a woman lacks understanding; he who does so destroys his own soul* (Proverbs 6:32).

The soul is the mind, the will, and the emotions. The person who commits sexual sin—adultery, infidelity, pornography—destroys his own soul. Over many years of pastoral ministry, I have often sat across the desk from men who are in captivity to either infidelity, pornography, or some other sexual sin. I would hear time after time, "Phil, I don't feel a thing." He didn't feel anything because he had brought death to his soul. It's the part of you that is meant to feel and think.

Sin can be so subtle and deceptive that it clouds your judgment to the point where you cannot think honestly and rationally. Sexual sin destroys the spiritual and emotional nerve receptors, so you can no longer feel what God intended you to feel. In 1 Timothy 4:2, the apostle Paul writes, *"...having their own conscience seared with a hot iron."*

I was badly burned on my leg as a teenager. The scar is barely visible today, but a small area on my calf is still numb because the nerves were destroyed, and I can't feel anything. Paul is warning that this happens to the human conscience—the soul—through repeated sin.

People have told me they are leaving their family and their spouse to marry their affair partner. They believe what they are doing is God's will for their lives. They've looked me in the eye with a straight face and said, "Well, Pastor Phil, we've been praying, and we believe we are the answer to each other's prayers. It was God who brought us together."

They are committing the sin of adultery. They are leaving their marriages, betraying their spouses, and breaking the vows they took before God on their wedding day. They are fracturing their families and deeply injuring and traumatizing their children. Yet they are convinced they are the answer to each other's prayers and that somehow God is the author of their relationship.

I have literally thought to myself while someone was telling me this, *Have you lost your mind?* Guess what. They have. They have brought death to their soul, and they can no longer think rationally. Because of their sin, they are under such deception that they really believe God is now affirming and endorsing their sin, as though they are the exception. When it comes to adultery, if they do it *with* you, they are proving they could do it *to* you. Yes, you may build a fire, but odds are it will blow up and blow out.

Sex outside of marriage can be exciting and full of intensity, but never, ever think intensity is the same as intimacy. Promiscuity, premarital sex, and extramarital sex might be exciting, but you were made for something more than intensity. You long for the intimacy that God created marriage to provide. Over the course of a decades-long marriage, there are times when sex will be hot, steamy, erotic, and passionate. But other times, it will cool off and ebb and flow. That's okay because you've built a fire that won't blow up and blow out. It's a fire that will last because it can be rekindled again and again.

Building a Fire

There's a right way and a wrong way to build a fire. When I get in a hurry and use a starter log and some newspaper, I have a blazing fire for only about five minutes because that's the wrong way to build a fire. That's why many couples who start having sex after the second date can't stand each other six months later. When you start a fire with kerosene and a match, it will burn fast and hot and then burn out.

I've learned how to start a fire the right way—one that will burn all day and into the night—with a hot bed of coals to rekindle the fire the next day. You must start it slowly with a hot bed of embers. You must have long-lasting fuel for the fire. When you do, it will burn hot, it will burn long, and it will last.

If you want to start a fire in your marriage that will go the distance, you cannot do it by simply throwing some kerosene on it and building your relationship on sex. That's what happens when couples choose the world's way instead of God's way and start sleeping together. They immediately jump into bed together and eventually even move in together before they are married.

If you want love to last a lifetime, you must start with a hot bed of coals. The best fires start slowly. I'm talking about stirring this love up carefully, methodically, and slowly, like Solomon and the Shulamite. Do it the right way, and the day you say, "I do," it is going to get hot. God wants you to have red-hot monogamous sex in marriage. Yes, God is right, and our present culture is wrong.

The best sex is married sex.

Solomon made the Shulamite feel like a cherished, precious Cinderella because of how he treated her. Like these two lovebirds from almost 3,000 years ago, developing those feelings begins before marriage while the relationship is still growing. Solomon made her feel honored and special. Men, one of the ways you make your lady feel treasured is to treat her with honor. Protect her virtue while you are dating, and your protection will carry over to your marriage long after the honeymoon is over. Trust me. When you make your wife feel treasured, she will say, "Get me some raisin cakes."

Here are some things to think about if you're single. How can you pursue a relationship in a healthy way by putting patience on the front end so you can have passion on the back end? How can you make sure you don't settle for less than God's best? Married or single, the first thing to do is repent of any sin in your life because it will rob you of God's best. What does it mean to repent? Repent means saying from your heart, "God, I am wrong, and You are right. I'm turning from sin and toward You."

True repentance leads to redemption and restoration.

If you have been taken captive by sexual sin, the first thing to do is repent. Regardless of how much or how long you have sinned, it is not too late for you. God loves you. The amazing thing about God's grace is that it is for you. God loves do-overs. He is the God of new beginnings. He is the God of second chances. When you repent of your sin, God hits the restart button.

I have counseled hundreds of couples getting ready for marriage. They have often told me, "We just want to be honest. We have not done this right. We have been sleeping together for the last three years, but we want God's best and to be blessed. We've promised each other and God that we will not sleep together again until we're married." If you have awakened that sexual passion too soon, it is not too late to repent.

Never Too Late

After you've repented, surrender everything to God, including your sexuality. Being a Christian means surrendering every part of your life to the Lord Jesus Christ. It is impossible to say, "I'm a follower of the Son of God, but I'm not a follower of the Word of God."

We now live in a "Christian" church culture that is increasingly antithetical to the core tenets of Christianity. Christianity in Western civilization looks increasingly like Christian paganism or atheism. Of course, those are oxymorons. There is no such thing, but my point is that we live in a time when professing Christians harmonize non-Christian beliefs and lifestyles with a counterfeit form of Christianity that contradicts following Christ.

When it comes to matters of gender and human sexuality, modern culture says anything goes. You can disagree with God, but I promise that God will not change His mind, even though our American society has changed its mind. It's not the purpose of God to align Himself with us, but rather our purpose is to align ourselves with Him. This is why the apostle Paul writes to early Christians living in a very similar culture of sexual depravity...

I beseech you therefore, brethren, by the mercies of God, that you present your bodies a living sacrifice, holy, acceptable to God, which is your reasonable service (Romans 12:1).

It is amazing how many Christians, both single and married, refuse to surrender and consecrate their sexuality to God. As a child of God, your body does not belong to you. It belongs to God. In the face of sexual temptation, Paul taught us to present our bodies as a living sacrifice to God. When we present our bodies to Him, it's impossible to present them to sin. You win in times of temptation by submission rather than suppression. You can't suppress sin; eventually, your willpower will fail. Instead, you must submit your will to God's will, which is for you to prosper and be healthy.

Beloved, I pray that you may prosper in all things and be in health, just as your soul prospers (3 John 2).

One of the most common lies of our modern society is "my body, my choice." Really? Did you create yourself or give life to yourself? Did you put breath or a beating heart in your own body? Of course not. Our bodies belong to God, who created us. As Christians, He has ransomed us. He has pardoned us and bought us with a price—the blood of Jesus Christ.

Or do you not know that your body is the temple of the Holy Spirit who is in you, whom you have from God, and you are not your own? For you were bought at a price; therefore glorify God in your body and in your spirit, which are God's (1 Corinthians 6:19-20).

You do not get to look at whatever you want; those eyes aren't yours. You do not get to say whatever you want; that mouth isn't yours. You do not get to listen to whatever you want; those ears aren't yours. You do not get to touch whatever you want; those hands aren't yours. You are to present every part of your body to God as a living sacrifice because it all belongs to Him. That also means you do not get to sleep with whomever you want, however you want.

A man once told me, "I want you to know that I have same-sex attraction, but because I'm a Christian, I choose to live in celibacy." That is what it means to be a Christian. Someone who pursues holiness is a true disciple and follower of Christ. That should be the attitude of every Christian regardless of the temptation. You surrender everything in your life for His glorification, even at the expense of your gratification. I have more respect for a man like that than the average American Christian male who says, "I'm a Christian," while he's secretly online looking at pornography at night while his wife is sleeping.

Dealing with Temptation

How do we deal with temptation? No matter how long you have been a Christian, every born-again child of God must deal with temptation every day. It's called "being human," and it's a part of our fallen human condition. One person's temptation is same-sex attraction. Another person's temptation is viewing pornography. Another person's temptation may be marital infidelity or fornication.

Temptation comes in many different forms, but you overcome it all in the same way: With a heart attitude of submission to a life of purity and holiness according to what God says and not what the world says. It is impossible to submit to sin when you submit to God and the eternal truths of His Word. Only when you refuse to submit to Him do you open the door to submit to sin. Make this your declaration every moment of every day:

Jesus, I surrender my will to You today for Your glory.

Next, put guardrails in your life. You can have the best intentions; you can really "mean it" this time and still not do it because it's not a matter of self-determination or how much willpower you think you have. You will eventually give in. That's why you need guardrails in your life. There is a reason the highway department puts guardrails anywhere there is a cliff or even a deep ditch. It's because getting too close to the edge is dangerous. Going over the edge can cost you your life.

Sin is dangerous. *"The wages of sin is death"* (Romans 6:23). You need guardrails because "going over the edge" morally will cost you your life, when Jesus wants you to have abundant life (John 10:10). If you are serious about living a life that is holy and brings God glory, you will put guardrails in your life. What is a guardrail in your walk with the Lord?

> *...make no provision for the flesh, to fulfill its lusts* (Romans 13:14).

This practical wisdom from God's Word simply means not giving yourself an opportunity to sin in the face of temptation. We all face temptation and opportunities to sin. Guardrails ensure that temptation and opportunity never intersect. Without them, sooner or later, you'll find yourself in the wrong place.

If you keep putting yourself in the wrong place—where temptation and opportunity intersect—eventually, you will do the wrong thing. If you have temptation but no opportunity, it's impossible to sin. If you have an opportunity but no temptation, you won't sin. Only when temptation and opportunity come together do they become a dangerous combination.

***Every Christian needs guardrails with practical boundaries
and accountability.***

You can put yourself in the wrong place after a night on the town when you invite your date in for a cup of coffee. Saying yes to the invitation can put you in the wrong place as well. Just coffee? Maybe. But it's the wrong place because temptation and opportunity will meet. The right place is saying goodnight at the door and concluding your evening by thanking God for keeping you pure. When you make the decision to stay out of the wrong places, it becomes difficult to do the wrong thing. Everyone needs guardrails, whether you are married or single.

One of my guardrails is to never, for any reason, be alone with a woman who is not my wife. We won't go to lunch alone, even though we are friends. I won't counsel a lady who needs pastoral advice alone behind closed doors. Sin begins subtly and innocently. Another guardrail in my life is making my email and internet activity open for review by a few members of my staff. Integrity seeks accountability. I never withhold my phone from my wife. She knows the passcode. She can pick it up and look at my texts and emails to see who I've been talking to. Integrity fosters trust. When you pursue integrity, you pursue accountability.

I trust God completely; I do not trust myself.

Those who are wise and spiritually mature have learned they can trust God completely but not themselves at all. If you are dating and pursuing marriage, you need to let somebody into your life who will ask you tough questions. How are you doing? Are you staying pure? Are you having trouble with pornography? There is no reason not to have a filter on your phone or computer. There are people in my life who I allow to ask me hard questions.

It's important not to stir up or awaken love before its time. This was the Shulamite's wise counsel to the "daughters of Jerusalem"—the single young ladies in her life. If you are dating with marriage in view, choose to limit physical affection in your relationship. Don't stir it up too soon. You will either fall into temptation or live in complete frustration. All it takes is one kiss to open the door to Satan's deceptions and devices. I'm not suggesting it's a sin to kiss the one you love, but two people in love don't naturally stop with one kiss. One kiss makes you want another kiss. That kiss leads to still another kiss.

The next thing you know, you're making out. And then... you get the point. I taught this principle to my kids for years before they ever started dating. People in love are not meant to stop once they start. A mature Christian couple in a relationship with marriage in view will decide together to limit how much physical affection they are willing to give each other.

Pursue wisdom in your relationships.

I was in middle school when I first held hands with a girl. It was at a church youth camp. We were outside on a starry summer night. Our pinkies touched, and my heart leaped. Our hands clasped. I got an adrenaline dump coursing through my body as my heart started racing. How exciting! It did not take long to realize that what was once exciting to me wasn't exciting anymore. Holding hands with a girl no longer made my heart race. It is a progression to passion.

If you want to limit physical affection, you will talk about your boundaries as a couple. Make the decision not to go past a certain point—one that is long before you've gone too far. Do that, and you'll pick the sweetest fruit on the vine as God intended. God loves you. He is not trying to keep you from something good. He wants to *give* you something far better than you ever dreamed possible. If you exercise patience as a single person, your reward will be a marriage of phenomenal passion. The choice is yours.

—— 5 ——

MORE THAN A FEELING

For all the singles *and* married couples reading this book, you need to understand that love is more than a feeling—it takes intention. Falling in love is easy; staying in love is a choice. As we trace our lovers' courtship, you'll see they are very intentional as singles who one day want to be married. They are an example of how to do it right. Do not just stumble around dating, hoping to find "the one." That seems to be the overarching methodology of our culture—hoping to get lucky and stumble into "the one" and have a happily-ever-after married life. *There is a better way!*

Falling in love is easy; staying in love is your choice.

If you want to be married and experience true intimacy, you need to date intentionally. Nothing happens accidentally or randomly. There is a four-part progression that leads to having a healthy, happy marriage until death do you part—dating with intention, courtship, engagement, marriage.

The first step is dating with intention. Most of the time when two people meet for the first time and think it is love at first sight, it is usually not love—it is infatuation. You cannot love someone you don't know. Now I don't want to minimize infatuation. All people who fall in love start out like this. That initial chemistry is an almost intangible and unexplainable mystery as to why two people fall in love. The problem is they have been taught by our society that love is a feeling. So, when they no longer feel the infatuation, they give up and move on to another relationship to start the process all over again. For an infatuation to progress to lasting love, it must be done with intention.

Most singles envision getting married at some point. If you are thinking intentionally and marriage is your destination, you will begin by asking yourself some questions openly and honestly. Ask yourself if you have the emotional and spiritual maturity to handle a romantic relationship.

Dating is a contact sport—people get hurt, and hearts get broken. The goal is for both people to make it to the altar with a healthy heart so they can have a healthy marriage. There are so many unhealthy marriages in our culture because there are so many spiritually and emotionally unhealthy married people. When two people have unhealthy hearts, their marriage will be unhealthy.

You also need to ask yourself if you have the maturity to date. Many people do not. If you are not sure, that's a good indicator that you need to wait. Perhaps you've just gone through a divorce. You've been through the drama and the trauma of a heart-wrenching loss in your life. The worst thing you can do with your hemorrhaging heart is to start dating and get right back into a relationship. You need to take some time to heal instead of looking for someone to help ease the pain you're experiencing.

Most of us have probably seen a teenage boy hanging on his girlfriend when walking through the mall. He has a content look on his face and a big hickey on his neck. You might have even thought to yourself, *That is a relationship brimming with promise.* I know what I'm talking about because I was that kid. I didn't have a clue about the train wreck that lay ahead. I had a can of kerosene, and she had a book of matches. Before it's over, chances are he will break a lot of hearts, and his heart will get broken, too. That was my story.

That is how I finally stumbled into "the one." Most of what I've learned about dating is from doing it all wrong. You may be thinking, *Pastor Phil, it looks like it worked out well for you. You and Christa have been married for over thirty years, and it looks like you're living happily ever after.* Yes, by the grace of God, it is going to be "happily ever after." Statistically, it should have been a different story with a different ending. God's grace wrote a different story over my life and marriage, but I still bear the scars of past sin.

I have many painful memories from my adolescence and young adult years when no one taught me to guard my heart. I took that unhealthy heart into my marriage, and sinful dysfunctional patterns plagued our early years together. That's why I'm telling you right now what I wish someone would have told me.

The goal is to marry with a whole and healthy heart.

Parents, this is why you need to have a plan to talk with your children early and often. Teach them how to navigate the teenage years so they will be ready for marriage when the time is right. The cultural methodology of random dating is nothing more than practicing for divorce and remarriage—out of one relationship and into the next and repeat.

Young people start dating years before they have the maturity for marriage. Random dating, especially without emotional maturity, only leads to temptation, frustration, drama, and trauma. Eventually, they will stumble to the altar with their hearts wounded and broken from years of failed relationships.

As parents, we think it's just part of growing up, but it doesn't have to be. Our job is to help our children navigate the dating and relationship minefield, even in the areas where, perhaps, we didn't do well, so they will be prepared for a happy marriage. If they do not have a healthy, whole heart when they get married, it's more difficult to have a healthy, happy marriage.

If you want to begin dating with marriage in mind, you need to have a profile of the kind of person you want to marry. Most dating websites ask you to do a compatibility test, which is really a personality profile. In their eyes, personality equals compatibility. Remember, this is not always true.

The most important aspects of compatibility have less to do with personality and everything to do with your values and worldview. Yes, personality matters in some capacity. Some people are attracted to the "life of the party" personality while others are attracted to the quieter "thinker" in the group. But more important than personalities are priorities. The things that matter most to your future spouse must matter to you. I don't mean their interests and hobbies, although I do think you should look for things to do together that you both enjoy. More importantly, that person should be someone who is earnestly pursuing Jesus, who has a heart of humility, and who isn't lazy.

> If the destination isn't marriage, then you're dating for the wrong reason.

Now you are thinking with intention because you have a destination. You are not just randomly going out for a good time. Too often, people fall in love with someone they never dreamed they would ever marry because you often fall in love with the people you hang out with. If this person doesn't fit the profile of somebody you want to marry, do not date or hang around them.

There must be a destination for dating other than just having fun. If the destination isn't marriage, then you're dating for the wrong reason. Does the profile you have in mind include the character qualities that are your non-negotiables?

Practically speaking, if you found "the one," are you ready for marriage, or are you still years away? If you are years away from being able to get married, then save yourself the drama, the trauma, the temptation, and frustration, and do not date. It is a waste of energy. If you are a guy, hang out with your buds. If you are a girl, hang out with your girlfriends. If you hang out with members of the opposite sex in a private setting, even if you are just talking, emotions will start to fly.

The next thing you know, you may want to get married, but you are years away from having the maturity necessary for marriage. This is why teenagers need to delay pursuing romantic relationships. What are you going to do if you fall in love at fourteen or fifteen years of age?

You can find an exception to everything. I recently met a couple who have been happily married for years, and they started dating in middle school. But this is the exception, not the norm. Wisdom says to wait until you are within striking distance of being able to get married. Then think about it from a practical standpoint.

Would you be financially able? You don't need a lot of money to get married, and you don't need a lot of money to start a life together. But it does take more money than many newlyweds think. Two cannot live together as cheaply as one unless one goes hungry and the other goes naked. Practically speaking, are you in a position financially and emotionally to get married? If not, you are far better off waiting.

Four Stages of Dating in View of Marriage

Once you decide you are ready to begin pursuing a relationship in view of marriage, there are four stages of progression that you must navigate with intention.

Friendship Stage

The first stage of dating is the *friendship* stage, which is for observation and edification. At some point, you progress beyond talking, and you have an interest in this person. At this stage, you are not asking them for promises they are not prepared to make. You are not asking them for a commitment to refrain from dating anybody else. There is no expectation in the relationship. You are just hanging out and getting to know each other.

At this stage of the dating process, you want to find out whether you agree theologically and philosophically. Remember, real compatibility is related to your most deeply held personal values and core convictions. While it's not essential that you agree on everything, it's vital to agree on the important things.

If you are a sold-out follower of Jesus, an atheist might make a great friend but not a marriage partner because you have two different worldviews. Somebody from another religion, such as Islam, Hinduism, or Buddhism might make a great neighbor, but certainly not a spouse. When you view God differently, you will view life differently, and you'll never enjoy the deepest levels of marital intimacy. If a Christian is married to an atheist, they can have a genuinely happy marriage together. However, it is less than ideal as intimacy is more than physical—it's spiritual as well.

Sometimes people get married, and they are not believers. One of them might hear the gospel and begin following Christ. Perhaps the other person becomes an atheist after marriage. The apostle Paul wrote specifically about this because so many pagans in the first century were coming to faith in Jesus while still married to an unbelieving spouse.

The Corinthians were asking Paul what they should do. Should they divorce their spouse since they were unequally yoked now to an unbeliever? Paul said, "No," unless the unbeliever wants to divorce them. His reasoning is that the believing spouse might influence the unbeliever toward Christ.

> *But to the rest I, not the Lord, say: If any brother has a wife who does not believe, and she is willing to live with him, let him not divorce her. And a woman who has a husband who does not believe, if he is willing to live with her, let her not divorce him. For the unbelieving husband is sanctified by the wife, and the unbelieving wife is sanctified by the husband; otherwise your children would be unclean, but now they are holy. But if the unbeliever departs, let him depart; a brother or a sister is not under bondage in such cases. But God has called us to peace. For how do you know, O wife, whether you will save your husband? Or how do you know, O husband, whether you will save your wife?* (1 Corinthians 7:12-16)

While a believing spouse should not divorce his or her spouse because they don't believe in Christ, the Bible is clear that it's still better to avoid this situation whenever possible. Amos 3:3 says, *"Can two walk together, unless they are agreed?"* Paul says in 2 Corinthians 6:14, *"Do not be unequally yoked together with unbelievers...."* If you are, you will never have the true depth of joy and intimacy in your marriage that God wants for you.

When you are dating somebody, you are already attracted to them outwardly, or you wouldn't be there. Dating is to get to know who they are inwardly. This assessment should not take more than a few months of dating to determine if they fit the profile or not. It should be a relatively quick process. If they do not have the potential for a future spouse, you need to go your separate ways.

The age-old question is, "Can guys and girls just be friends?" The answer is no, especially once you've dated. Yes, you can be casual friends, but attempting to be close, personal friends will eventually result in one, if not both, beginning to fall in love.

When one of you is not in love and the other one is, it leads only to heartbreak. Protect your heart and theirs by not trying to be just friends. You can be Facebook friends. You can be casual friends. You can be "we hang out together in a crowd" kind of friends. But attempting to be close, intimate friends is not guarding your heart or theirs. Wisdom says to do the hard thing—walk away and close the door behind you.

Courtship

On the other hand, after a few months, you might realize this person has potential, and you might even feel like the two of you are starting to fall in love. At this point, the relationship needs to be redefined as the second stage, *courtship*. I know there are those who don't like this term, so call it whatever you want. Call it the "dating, but more than friends" stage. It doesn't matter what you call it, but you are no longer dating for edification and observation. Your relationship has progressed to the stage where you need to clearly define the relationship.

Now, you are asking for a commitment to see each other exclusively in view of marriage. You are not yet engaged. You haven't bought the ring. You haven't set any dates to send out the wedding invitations. But you are now seeing each other in a committed, exclusive relationship. You agree not to see anyone else. It is the same progression we see in Solomon and the Shulamite's relationship.

During this stage, it is important to get to know each other's family. Even though God says in Genesis 2:24, *"A man shall leave his father and mother and be joined to his wife,"* you are, in effect, marrying their family as well. Much of a person's upbringing and family of origin have deeply shaped them into who they are. That is why it's important to get to know your potential spouse's family roots and heritage.

I told you the story of Christa and me at the beginning of this book. By now, you know that I worked hard to make her my high school sweetheart. That didn't work out, but all that work paid off in college when we became sweethearts. We had a long-distance relationship during our first year of college. We attended different universities a couple hundred miles away from each other.

This was back in the days of long-distance telephone bills, and I remember selling my blood plasma every month to pay for the phone calls. Those were also the days of hand-written love letters to each other, mailed in a real envelope that was not expected to reach its destination for days. Cell phones, direct messaging, and texting have changed the dating game.

After dating long-distance during our first semester of college, our relationship clearly progressed by Christmas break. Yes, as predicted, there were lots of other girls on campus. I'd met quite a few nice young ladies who were very pretty as well. However, after seeing Christa in person only a few times that fall, I realized the "new girl with the pretty green eyes" was still the only one who captured my thoughts and, ultimately, my heart. Somehow, along the way, I captured hers as well.

That is when we both knew we wanted to get married someday, and we officially redefined the relationship as an *exclusive, committed* relationship. I knew she was "the one" I wanted to marry. And I knew she felt the same. We had arrived at the stage when you begin dating each other's family and not just each other.

I remember spending time with her family over Christmas break—and having the eye-opening realization of what it meant to marry into a German Lutheran family with a culture of its own. It was quite different from the family culture in which I grew up. While we both strayed far from Jesus in our teens, we were both raised in Christian families. However, our denominational traditions were very different.

I first noticed how her devout Lutheran dad drank beer and wine. I was truly shocked to see real wine served with Christmas dinner. This may sound humorous to you, but in the conservative Christian home I grew up in, I honestly didn't know Christians could do that. I've since concluded that one can have a beer and still love Jesus. But I'll never forget the first time I went to church with Christa, and she returned to her seat next to me after taking communion and had alcohol on her breath. What?! Real wine? This would never happen at my church, where communion was taken with grape juice.

The real issue we had to work through was after we both began passionately following Jesus and discovered our different beliefs about baptism. Her tradition taught infant baptism. She had been christened as a baby. Mine taught believers' baptism—only baptizing people after they made Jesus the Lord of their lives. This may not sound like a big issue, but it's far better discussed and decided ahead of time rather than years into your marriage after your first baby is born. This would become an ongoing discussion, debate, occasional argument, and, dare I say, "fight" over the coming months. Thank God we eventually had enough sense to settle it with the Bible.

I spent lots of time with her family over Christmas break, playing cards and board games. I was raised in a family that never played cards, probably because that's the way my mother was raised. I didn't even know any card games, and I considered board games to be "bored" games, but I was having fun with Christa and her family.

And while I was checking them out, they were undoubtedly doing the same to me. It turns out they had already given me their vote of approval, which Christa told me later. We would eventually travel with her family to the small farming town in Illinois where her dad was raised and where I had the privilege of meeting her German Lutheran grandmother—a precious lady I miss to this day.

I eventually took Christa to southern Missouri, where she met the "country" side of my family. I took her to the farm where my dad grew up before moving to Kansas City as a young man to find work. I wanted her to meet my Grandma and Grandpa Hopper, who were so influential in my life. Some of my favorite memories are times spent on my granddad's farm. It was my home away from home in the summer while growing up. I wanted my city-born and bred girlfriend to know she was marrying a city kid who was also half-country. Those memories were part of my identity, and I wanted her to know every part of me. Getting to know each other's family reveals a lot about your identity.

As you date, you discover each other's true character qualities. The infatuation you felt initially begins to wear off. Only then can you see someone for who they really are, and only then can you begin to love them for who they really are. *You didn't choose to fall in love, but now you're choosing to stay in love.*

Infatuation distorts reality and convinces you the person is amazing and the perfect human being. Anybody can get religion just long enough to get married. Anybody can be on their best behavior for two hours on a date. Time tests everything, including how they respond when they are tired or stressed and how they act when there's a disagreement. Do you still see humility, or do you see selfishness? When someone is squeezed, you see who they really are at their very core. You don't get to see that the first time you go on a date because they are putting their best foot forward.

Define your future together.

It is during the courtship stage that you define the future for your family, your finances, and your faith. You might want to find out ahead of time if one of you wants at least twelve children and the other doesn't want more than two. Perhaps one is a saver and the other a spender. As I said before, you don't need a lot of money, but you do need to have a plan. The subject of finances is one of the biggest stresses in every marriage. Knowing where you are going and having a plan to get there will eliminate financial stress after you're married.

Talk about your faith and what it means to you. Discuss how you want to use your faith together to advance the Great Commission and take the gospel to all nations. If she is called to world missions and wants to live her life in India, and he never wants to leave his hometown, they have a problem.

There are things you will learn about each other during your courtship that you couldn't learn any other way. Before the wedding, you need to talk about and define the roles, responsibilities, and expectations for your relationship. You might see yourself in a traditional marriage with more traditional roles. Maybe he wants to marry a woman who will be a stay-at-home mom and take care of the kids. On the other hand, she may be career-minded and want upward mobility. These things are not necessarily mutually exclusive. But they are things to discover ahead of time to determine how they will impact your relationship as husband and wife.

Our society is trying to rock the roles of men and women that have been set by God. Ephesians 5 tells us that the husband is to be a picture of Christ, and the wife, a picture of the Church. Those are immutable roles set in place by a loving God for eternity.

On the other hand, responsibilities can differ from one marriage to another. For example, in our marriage, I am responsible for doing the yard work and taking care of the outside of the house. Yet Christa and I know other couples where the wife loves doing yard work, including mowing the lawn. There is nothing wrong with that. These are not roles; they are responsibilities. While I didn't do a lot of inside housework in the early days of our marriage, today I do a lot of dishes and even vacuum and mop the floors. No, I still don't do a lot of laundry, but I'm getting better at that too. It's okay either way because these are responsibilities, and they can change over time.

Discuss your shared responsibilities ahead of time.

It is vitally important to discuss your shared responsibilities ahead of time. Sometimes, they go unspoken, but if you don't decide on them ahead of time, you might have some disagreements that could have been avoided. Unspoken and unmet expectations are a source of frustration. Much of how we view responsibilities in marriage between husbands and wives has to do with what was modeled for us growing up. Talk about it in this stage of your relationship, and your transition from single to married will be much smoother.

If you are convinced you have found "the one," your courtship shouldn't take longer than six months to a year at the most. If you have been with somebody for a year and still don't know if you want to marry them, you need to call it what it is and end it. The longer you delay, the harder it's going to be to bring closure. The more time you have invested in the relationship, the more difficult it becomes to walk away. Either you want to marry the person, or you don't.

I am not an advocate for lengthy courtships because I don't believe the Bible teaches it. Paul says in 1 Corinthians 7:9, *"...it is better to marry than to burn with passion."* Courting or dating for years and being engaged for even more is setting yourself up for temptation and frustration. Don't burn with passion, or you will not make it to the altar with a whole, healthy heart and with your purity and integrity intact. If after a year, you know you are in love and share the same values for your future and your family, then set a date and prepare to get married.

Engagement

The third stage of the progression to marriage is *engagement.* There are several things that must be addressed during your engagement, including wedding plans and plans to set up a home together. But there is seldom a reason why a lengthy engagement is required. My mother and father were married almost six months from the day they met. Their marriage lasted more than 55 years until the death of my mother. If you've dated or courted well, a lengthy engagement shouldn't be necessary. There is not a lot of explanation needed about this phase of your relationship. Pick a date. Pick a location. Make the plans. And let the wedding bells ring!

Marriage

It all culminates in the fourth stage of the relationship, which is *marriage*—a covenant relationship until death do you part. Jesus says in Matthew 19:6, *"What God has joined together, let not man separate."* People think of marriage as a contractual agreement. A fundamental problem in modern society is that in the eyes of God, marriage is not a contract as many tend to view it—it's a covenant.

A contract can be terminated because it's based on terms and conditions. If the terms aren't met, the contract can be broken. It's built on a conditional agreement that says if the other party does their part, then I'll do my part. But if at any point they fail to meet the terms of the contract, I can walk away.

On the other hand, a covenant is binding, unbreakable, irrevocable, and irreversible. Remember, in God's eyes, marriage is meant to be a picture of the covenant relationship between Christ and His bride. Jesus says as the Bridegroom, *"I will never leave you nor forsake you"* (Hebrews 13:5).

It is important for couples to see marriage as a covenant. You see, I can promise through the course of a decades-long marriage, your spouse will hurt you, offend you, disrespect you, disappoint you, and completely let you down. Sometimes your spouse will act self-centered and selfish, if not downright sinful. They will put themselves first when they promise to put you first. They will think about their own needs when they promise to think about your needs.

If you see marriage as a contract, there will be a point when you will convince yourself you have a right to walk away. The covenant promise Jesus makes in Hebrews 13:5 is that even if you walk away from Him, He will never walk away from you. It's not conditional on what you do or don't do but on what He said and did. That is the picture of your marriage He wants to paint to a watching world.

We've defined what constitutes a biblical divorce in God's eyes, but divorce is not always a sin. Sometimes a marriage can't be saved. You don't have to stay in a marriage with a repeat adulterer, abuser, or someone who has abandoned you. Jesus taught the grounds for biblical divorce in Matthew 19, and Paul added to it in 1 Corinthians 7.

A successful marriage requires commitment from *both* of you. If your spouse refuses to repent of his or her sin, you can't save your marriage by yourself. But often, the marriage could have been saved if it had been built on a covenant relationship instead of a contract.

When Christa and I took our vows and said, "I do," we knew it was for life. We've never allowed the possibility of divorce to enter our minds, even at our lowest points along the way. We decided ahead of time that divorce would never be an option.

In the church I pastor, we celebrate marriages that have gone the distance—many lasting as long as 50 and 60 years. For all of them, there have been some difficult moments along the way when they would have preferred to leave. It all begins with your outlook on marriage. There is no back door. There is no exit. You took a vow before God, and you committed to keeping it.

Today, a lot of people, even professing Christians, get divorced with no biblical grounds. They say it's because they no longer love their spouse. I've heard them say through the years, "Pastor Phil, we just fell out of love." Okay, get over it and fall back in love. In a 50-year marriage, you are going to fall in and out of love many times. But love is more than a feeling. Love is a choice; it's a commitment.

You will have seasons of infatuation even in your fifties. I promise your best sex is not in your twenties. You will have moments of passion clear into your sixties and beyond. Some of your best moments as a married couple will come in the second half of your journey together. If you are growing and maturing as individuals and as a couple, marriage only gets better the older you become.

There will be seasons when it feels as though your love is waning, but that doesn't mean you don't still have love. You may have fallen out of love because you stopped doing the things that made you fall in love. Do those things again, and you can be head over heels in love again. You don't get a divorce just because you have fallen out of love, or none of us would stay married.

Love is not always better the second time around. I'm not saying you can't find love the second time around, but you will now have to deal with your new spouse's baggage from their first marriage, and they will have to deal with yours.

You are going to have to deal with ex-spouses, fractured relationships, somebody else's kids and their grandkids, and how to handle it when your kids spend the weekend in someone else's home who doesn't share your values or parenting philosophy. You will have to deal with child custody and co-parenting. You're going to have to deal with how to handle money. You will have to deal with seeing your ex-spouse at your kid's soccer match every weekend with his or her new boyfriend or girlfriend. That awkward situation will follow you to every birthday party, holiday family gathering, wedding, and funeral. In a lot of ways, love is not better the second time around.

I pray you find it if God wills that for you. But if you are married, you have a lot of incentive to stay married. It is not necessarily going to be better the second time around, and it will definitely be more difficult.

Guard your relationship from the little foxes.

Whether you are single and would like to be married, dating someone in view of marriage, or already married, it is important that you learn how to protect your relationship from the little foxes that spoil tender love.

Catch us the foxes, the little foxes that spoil the vines, for our vines have tender grapes (Song of Solomon 2:15).

In Song of Solomon chapter 1, we learn that the Shulamite has lost her sexual purity. Her brothers were so angry that they made her work outside in the sun. Now that she is in a relationship with Solomon, her brothers tell her to *"make sure you catch those little foxes that spoil the tender grapes"*—a euphemism for tender love before it has fully matured.

At that time, everybody had a vineyard. It was a common occurrence for foxes to creep into the vineyard at night and gnaw on the roots of the grapevines. Of course, the vine would start to erode, and the fruit would dry up. Other times, they would nip and pick at the tender grapes for moisture. It was a very arid part of the world, and they were thirsty. The brothers warned their sister to guard against the little foxes who would attempt to steal her love before it fully matured. Whether you are in a marriage or courting, we all need to guard our relationships from the little foxes.

When you are a single man or woman, there are many things to consider to protect your relationship as it progresses. Spend time dating publicly as Solomon and the Shulamite did at the very end of chapter 1. In verses 16 and 17, she says, *"Behold, you are handsome, my beloved! Yes, pleasant! Also our bed is green. The beams of our houses are cedar, and our rafters of fir."*

She describes a couch of green grass with fir trees as the rafters of their abode. They are relaxing together outside. Not inside. They are on a date in a very public setting rather than spending time privately without prying eyes. They are protecting their virtue and integrity as a couple. They are practicing one of the guardrails of accountability by not allowing temptation and opportunity to intersect.

You can still enjoy conversations together, share an intimate dinner in a restaurant, stroll through a shopping mall, or any other shared activity. But the more time you spend together privately, the more opportunities you have for temptation to sin. You open the door to the little foxes, spoiling the vine of your relationship. Solomon and the Shulamite made sure to spend time together where others could see them. Follow their example to protect yourself and your reputation and ensure the integrity of your relationship.

Next, let God be the architect of your character. In chapter 2, verse 1, the Shulamite compares herself to two very common flowers in her part of the world—the rose of Sharon and the lily of the valleys. Her real beauty is her humility—she's anything but common. What's attractive about a beautiful woman is when she doesn't walk around flaunting her beauty.

It is the same with men. A handsome man is really handsome when he doesn't walk around like he is God's gift to women. We live in the ultimate selfie society that promotes self-idolatry and encourages us to seek attention and be idolized by others. Our lives should draw attention to Jesus, not ourselves.

While you are single, let God forge these character qualities in you, with humility being the first, followed by integrity, tenacity, and serving others selflessly. Use your time while single to become the one who you're looking for is looking for. Become that one. You will find each other as you become increasingly Christlike in your personal lives.

> If you don't learn to practice mental integrity while single, you won't have integrity in marriage either.

Also, don't randomly date. In verse 2, Solomon assures his bride-to-be that she is special and beautiful, *"like a lily among thorns,"* and he only has eyes for her. Solomon makes it clear that while there are many "flowers" in the field, he is not picking one flower while he is smelling all the others and playing the field. He is not dating around hoping to stumble into the right one. He is intentional in his actions.

As a single person, it is crucial you learn to discipline your mind to have integrity. While you are in a committed and exclusive dating relationship, do you continually have "wandering eyes"—mentally playing the field, hanging on to one flower while surveying all the others? That type of behavior does not automatically end just because you say, "I do." You have trained yourself over years of dating to always survey the field.

If you don't learn to practice mental integrity while single, you won't have integrity in marriage either. Now is the time to start training your mind—before you get married. Start thinking like you are married with an "I'm off the market" mindset and don't look for a better option. Dating until someone better comes along is not how you end up with a healthy marriage.

Next, create safety and security. In verses 3 and 4, the Shulamite says,

> *Like an apple tree among the trees of the woods, so is my beloved among the sons. I sat down in his shade with great delight, and his fruit was sweet to my taste. He brought me to the banqueting house, and his banner over me was love.*

In chapter 1, she was ashamed because she had been out in the sun and carried the stigma of her sin on her skin. In this man's presence, it was like living in the shade, shielded from the harshness and heat of the sun. Solomon has shielded her and made her feel protected. Then she said, "He brought me to the banqueting house." He pulled her chair out so she could sit with him at the king's table in a place of honor. Not only that, but she said, "His banner over me was love."

Banner is a military term. Armies went into battle with a banner so they could all see where to come together. It is also one of the names of God: Jehovah Nissi—God our banner. It means God goes to battle for us. She is saying that this man loves her enough to fight for her. He will go to battle for her and lay down his life for her. You can see why she is falling in love with him. She feels safe with him because he is intentionally creating a sense of security in their relationship.

You also need to commit to sexual purity. *"Do not stir up nor awaken love until it pleases"* (Song of Solomon 2:7). They promised each other they would not awaken the sexual part of their relationship before its time. They were making the decision not to let temptation and opportunity intersect. Limit physical affection, and do not awaken that part of your relationship until you are married.

Last, commit to getting to know each other deeply and intimately. In verse 8, Solomon takes the Shulamite on a date, and she says, *"The voice of my beloved! Behold, he comes leaping upon the mountains, skipping upon the hills."* Solomon is saying, "I am in love, and I do not care who knows it!" She sees him coming with a skip in his step, leaping up the mountains. In true Hebrew poetry fashion, she is thinking back on this time in the relationship, recalling how beautiful it was in verse 9:

> *My beloved is like a gazelle or a young stag. Behold, he stands behind our wall; he is looking through the windows, gazing through the lattice.*

They are having a playful moment, and Solomon is looking through the windows. He has just come to her house, and she does not yet know he is there. And he is saying, "I see you." He is flirting with her.

Rise Up! The Bridegroom Comes!

Beginning in verse 10 is a picture of the Rapture. The bridegroom is going to return one day and say to His bride, the Church, *"Rise up, my love, my fair one, and come away. For lo, the winter is past, the rain is over and gone. The flowers appear on the earth*"—speaking of the millennial kingdom. "*The time of singing has come, and the voice of the turtledove*"—the Holy Spirit—"*is heard in our land. The fig tree puts forth her green figs.*" In the parable of the fig tree, Jesus spoke of the rebirth of Israel.

In verse 14, Solomon says to the love of his life, "*O my dove, in the clefts of the rock, in the secret places of the cliff, let me see your face, let me hear your voice.*" It is the nature of a dove to stay in the clefts of the rock where there is safety. Solomon is saying, "Come out here because I want to see the secret places of your life. Let me be your source of safety."

True intimacy is unguarded intimacy.

This passage is a foreshadow of Jesus, the Rock of our salvation. He is a sure and eternal Refuge and the Foundation on which the hope of Heaven rests. "*...and he who believes on Him will by no means be put to shame*" (1 Peter 2:6). As a married person, you'll find your security in each other, but you'll never stop finding your security in Him. You get to know each other deeply as you begin to form this relationship of trust and security. That's when you begin to truly fall in love because you are sharing each other's secrets and the secret places of your lives. If you will take this time in your life to build your life on *the Rock,* whose name is Jesus, one day God just might give you a marriage that is never on the rocks.

─── 6 ───

HIS NEEDS, HER NEEDS

In Song of Solomon chapter 2, the lovebirds are beginning a new phase in their courtship. They are getting to know each other on a much deeper level. It is important to understand that men and women are equal but not the same physically or emotionally. God has made us unique as men and women (Genesis 1:27). While we are equal before God and created in His image, He created us as male and female.

Our society will argue that the differences in behavior between men and women are nothing more than the influence of social constructs, and men and women are essentially the same. Since it's God and not culture who created male and female, He gets the final say. While men and women are similar, we're clearly not the same. There are most certainly similarities and overlaps between the emotional needs of men and women, but our needs are different. When we fail to recognize our differences, it often leads to great disappointment.

In marriage, we need to learn each other's basic needs and how God made us—this is fundamental, Marriage 101, and essential to marital intimacy and happiness.

What we are going to learn from Solomon and his beautiful *"lily among thorns"* is that men are made by God to feel strong, and women are made by God to feel beautiful. A woman will naturally celebrate beauty while men will naturally celebrate strength. Women can be both beautiful and strong, and men can certainly appreciate both beauty and strength. Some of the greatest artists in history have been men, and some of the strongest leaders in history have been women. But the emotional needs of men and women, while similar, are not really the same.

We learn from Solomon and the Shulamite about the deepest longings within the hearts of men and women and how they fall in love and stay in love. This is important to understand because every human being has an emotional bank account. With every conversation and interaction, we are either making deposits or withdrawals from each other's bank accounts.

People fall in love with each other when deposits are consistently being made. In chapter 2, Solomon and the Shulamite fall in love because they are intentionally making many deposits into each other's accounts. Men and women fall out of love when those same accounts become overdrawn.

When we think about marital intimacy, most people will immediately think about what happens in the bedroom behind closed doors. You do not get real sexual intimacy until you get intimacy that takes place in the heart and mind. Marital sexual intimacy is simply the overflow of marital intimacy emotionally, spiritually, and mentally. *Intimacy* can be defined as "in-to-me-see." You will never know the depths of joy and intimacy sexually if you don't have the intimacy of heart and mind—the soul and the spirit.

Deepest-Level Connection

This couple is learning about each other's deepest needs throughout their courtship. They are not yet married, but they are connecting on a deeper level. As a pastor, I have counseled many married couples, and often a recurring pattern of dysfunction is a source of pain and strain.

For a marriage to be healthy, husbands and wives must learn how to meet each other's deepest needs. It is not some revelation we download the moment we say, "I do." We will naturally try to love our spouse the way we want to be loved. The way men feel loved and the way women feel loved are similar but, again, not the same.

Ephesians 5:33 gives us a clue. Women long for affection, while men long for admiration. It's not that men don't need affection and women don't need admiration. It's about how God has fundamentally made them feel loved by the other.

The Bible says in Matthew 19:6, *"What God has joined together, let not man separate."* Getting married is easy. Having a marriage that lasts a lifetime is costly, and it is certainly not easy. It demands learning and maturing both as a couple and individually. When I look back at that younger Phil, I realize I didn't have a clue what I was getting into. I didn't really know what to do. Nobody told me ahead of time. I knew I loved my wife, but it didn't take long for me to realize that I didn't know how to love her. Truthfully, she didn't really know how to love me either, though she was certain she loved me.

Who wants to be a flower, and who wants to be a stag?

The Shulamite compares herself to two very common flowers—the Rose of Sharon and the Lily of the Valley. She knows she is pretty, but not prettier than any of the other young women. Solomon quickly corrects her, saying, *"Like a lily among thorns, so is my love among the daughters."*

Solomon was not dubbed the wisest man who ever lived for nothing. He understood that he needed to recognize her beauty and make sure she knew that among all the other flowers, she stood apart and captured his heart. This man is making major emotional deposits.

Historically, men bring a bouquet of flowers as a special gift for the woman they love. Flowers, by nature, are beautiful, and when presented to a woman, they can make her feel beautiful. This interaction gives us a glimpse into the longing of a woman's heart and the need to be somebody's Cinderella—beautiful, special, and cherished. This is the most important need God has given a woman, specifically for her husband to meet. Unless the husband recognizes that need, he cannot meet his wife's needs. He may love her, but she won't feel loved. She longs to feel beautiful and special.

His and Hers

We live in a society that is increasingly trying to make men like women and women like men. But even the secular movie and entertainment industry understands the differences between male and female audiences and knows how to capitalize on them.

As the father of a little girl and two little boys, it was evident from the time they were very young that they didn't like watching the same movies. I would have to referee between *Superman* and *Batman* or *Snow White* and *Cinderella*. Society says we are all the same, but equal-ness is not same-ness. Men and women are equal but most definitely not the same. You can see the differences in the movies and cartoons they begin to gravitate toward from the earliest moments of a child's life—long before any social constructs have had time to shape their behavior. Just walk up to any man or woman and ask them to name their top three all-time favorite movies. Chances are they won't be sharing the same list.

This pattern is repeated in various ways, even when little girls grow up and become women. Whenever I've accompanied my wife to gatherings where all the ladies are wearing beautiful dresses, they greet each other by complimenting their attire and talking about how beautiful they look. You'll never catch men greeting each other saying things like, "Oh, you look so handsome. Did you change your hair? I love the way that shirt looks on you." No, on the contrary! I recently saw an old friend I hadn't seen in some time. The first words out of his mouth were, "Hey, there's the ugliest man I've ever seen." I wasn't offended. That's just guy talk for "Hey, I've missed seeing you."

> The heart of every woman longs not only to feel beautiful but to create beauty as well.

It's the same concerning where men and women live and how they decorate their surroundings. Women often decorate with beauty, while men tend to decorate with achievement. Single men often do not decorate at all. If they do, it is likely with old trophies from high school. On the other hand, women want to make their homes beautiful. A married man might have a man cave in a remote corner of the house that he decorates with sports memorabilia. The things he displays reveal how he is made. He is celebrating accomplishments. He is not displaying beauty but rather achievement.

When Christa and I go to someone's house for dinner, it almost always goes something like this: We greet each other at the door, and immediately the wife says to Christa, "Hey, follow me to the kitchen. I want to show you my new countertops," or, "Come and see my new kitchen cabinets." Not one time has a husband beckoned me to come to the kitchen to show me the new countertops and cabinets. On the contrary, I usually follow him downstairs to his man cave so he can show me a deer head with big antlers or a big fish hanging on the wall. In the end, we are all just boys and girls in adult bodies. It's how God created us.

The heart of every woman longs not only to feel beautiful but to create beauty as well. She longs for others, and especially the man in her life, to see and affirm her beauty. Husbands, this is why you may come home from work, and your wife greets you at the door saying, "Look around. Do you notice anything different?" You have that deer in the headlights look, and you are praying, "Please, Jesus, show me what's different." She wants you to affirm the beauty she has created. You are looking into the heart of your wife. The apostle Peter understood this, as a married man, when he wrote in 1 Peter 3:7:

> *Husbands, likewise, dwell with them with understanding, giving honor to the wife, as to the weaker vessel, and as being heirs together of the grace of life, that your prayers may not be hindered.*

Husband, do you understand your wife? Do you know her intimately and emotionally? Most men do not. Peter is not speaking negatively about women. He is saying that you need to study your wife with the same passion you would study ESPN highlights, stats for your fantasy football league, or how to improve your golf game. It takes work to truly know and understand the heart of your wife.

Women are commonly offended by the notion that they are the weaker vessel when they don't understand what Peter is really saying. This is not only a reference to the fact that women are typically smaller and physically weaker than their male counterparts. A weaker vessel was something to be cherished. He's teaching that men are to place a higher value on women than even themselves, and especially their wives. A vessel in Peter's time was a piece of ceramic pottery. The stronger vessels were commonplace and used for everyday purposes. They were not easily broken, but when they did, they were discarded.

Pieces of broken pottery can be found by the thousands to this day in ancient archaeological sites of the Holy Land. The weaker vessels were used to create beauty, and more time was taken to craft them. Think of a weaker vessel as a piece of fine china that would only be used on special occasions. Think how you would treat a priceless ceramic vase from the Ming Dynasty if you had possession of it. You would put it on a pedestal. You would handle it with care because it's priceless and something to be cherished.

The Feminine Heart

Even the ancient fairy tale *Snow White* recognizes the longing of the feminine heart. "Mirror, mirror on the wall, who is the fairest one of all?" Every woman, in some way, asks that question every day, and the most important mirror in her life is the most significant male in her life. "Does he see me? Am I special to him? Of all the other flowers in the world, does he think I am the most beautiful?" It begins when that little girl is still very young.

When my daughter was just a little girl, we returned home from a wedding where she was the flower girl. She was beaming at her reflection in the mirror and began twirling in her ruffly white dress. She didn't know I was watching her. Then she looked at me, and I will never forget how she began to twirl for me. I became her mirror saying, "You are beautiful and special."

My wife got out her wedding dress so Makay could dress up like she was the bride. Little boys don't dress up like bridegrooms. They don't want to wear a wedding tux just for fun or to dream of their wedding day. Little girls do. They love pretending they are a bride, and that should tell us something about the heart of a woman. Little girls dream about the day when they get to become somebody's Cinderella—when she gets to be the bride, and her groom looks at her and says, "You are beautiful and special." As a little girl, that man is her father. When she grows up and marries, that little girl is still in her, but the mirror is now her husband.

As husbands and fathers, we need to follow Solomon's example to ensure the women in our lives know that in our eyes, all the other flowers are like thorns. How a man expresses his love will make her feel beautiful or like just another flower. This is how God made a woman and the reason He put her in your life. She will fall in love and stay in love with a man who makes her feel beautiful and special.

You may have thought she married you because you were so good-looking that she couldn't resist. But the real reason may not be what you look like but how you made her feel—beautiful, special, and like someone to be treasured.

There's a reason the story of Cinderella has been around for so long. The longing it reveals is hardly the result of a modern American social construct of a misogynistic culture built on male patriarchy. Linguists and those who study ancient literature tell us it originated 1,000 years ago in China—passed down from culture to culture, continent to continent, and generation to generation about the longing in a woman's heart.

The Masculine Heart

Now on to the longing of a man's heart. Wise is the wife who understands it. The Shulamite certainly did.

> *My beloved is mine, and I am his. He feeds his flock among the lilies. Until the day breaks and the shadows flee away, turn, my beloved, and be like a gazelle or a young stag upon the mountains of Bether* (Song of Solomon 2:16-17).

In verse 16, she understands his needs are different from her needs and assures him that he is number one in her eyes. All of chapter 2 has been about their courtship. She is sharing a memory of this wonderful day they've spent together. As night descends in verse 17, she refers to the mountains of Bether that do not exist anywhere in the world. *Bether* means "separation, cutting, or cleavage." In Song of Solomon, it is a metaphor for her breasts. She was saying that it was time for them to part ways because she wasn't letting him near the mountains of Bether. Well done, future bride. She tells him when the dawn breaks, they can hang out some more.

Before she sends him on his way, she calls him a gazelle and a stag. What man doesn't want to be called a stag? She is wise and knows how a man ticks. Solomon has told her she's *"like a lily among thorns,"* the most beautiful flower of all the flowers of the field.

She doesn't return his compliment by calling him a beautiful flower. No, men don't care to be identified as flowers. They don't long to be beautiful. Men long to be strong and have their women affirm the strength they see in them. She calls him a stag because that's the language of men.

This is a virtuous woman who has committed herself to sexual chastity until she is married. But she doesn't emasculate her man. She knows a man needs some swag. Our culture has worked hard to emasculate men—but not this woman. She wants her man to be both happy and healthy, and she knows he won't be healthy or happy if she makes him feel weak. He needs to feel strong and longs for her to affirm his strength.

A man has two mirrors in his life—his woman and his work. Every day, in some way, he says, "Mirror, mirror on the wall, am I man enough at all? Am I strong enough?" A man will naturally retreat from any mirror that makes him feel weak. He may begin throwing himself more into his work or hobbies after years of marriage rather than his wife and his home. He will gravitate to whatever mirror makes him feel like a winner.

Ladies, a man will fall in love and stay in love with a woman who makes him feel strong and good about his masculinity. Yes, he was drawn to your looks because he is a visual creature. But he fell in love with you because of how you made him feel. Like Solomon's bride, you made him feel like a stag. A stud. You made him feel strong. It's an emotional need, and it's crucial every wife understands that and responds.

God has put strength in every man just as He has put beauty in every woman. Unfortunately, because of the fallen, sinful hearts within men, civilization abounds with accounts of strong men who were also bad men—using their strength to dominate women and prey on the weak.

Consequently, our society has equated *strong* men with *bad* men. It's now assumed all masculinity is toxic. To eliminate bad men, our modern society has attempted to make all men weak. The problem is you don't eliminate bad men by eliminating strong men. Otherwise, all that's left are weak men who aren't strong enough to deal with the bad men. It's time to bring back some biblical masculinity to American society.

Gentleman, God made you strong. It's time to stop denying it, avoiding it, letting others talk us out of it, and sometimes even apologizing for it. This is who we are because it's how God made us. A man's strength has nothing to do with how much he can bench press—it's about his heart. That strength is not meant to prey on the weak but to protect the weak. It's not meant to dominate a woman but rather serve her, even laying down his life for a woman like Christ did for the Church (Ephesians 5:25). Toxic masculinity is life-taking; biblical masculinity is life-giving. This is the biblical pattern we see emerging in the relationship between Solomon and the Shulamite.

Passion and Purity

Solomon is not one to take something for himself that is not yet his to take. He is giving life to the woman he loves, not taking life from her for his own sinful self-interests. True love doesn't take—it only gives. Song of Solomon is a record of this couple's passion as well as their purity. As you will see, they are passionate on the latter end because they are committed to purity on the front end. Most of us did not get this concept right in the beginning.

At one time, I was prodigal Phil, not Pastor Phil. I did things I wish I could change. There was a time in my life when I wasn't committed to sexual purity. I want to assure anyone who can relate to my story that there is redemption and restoration. Do not feel like you have blown it forever if you have slept around or done things you regret. Jesus can make all things new, and He can do that for you.

> *Therefore, if anyone is in Christ, he is a new creation; old things have passed away; behold, all things have become new* (2 Corinthians 5:17).

The only question is whether you want to be made new or continue the way you are. God can hit a restart button for you, whether you are single or married. I don't know where you've been or what you've done, but God promises redemption when you come to Him with a repentant heart. He can bring reconciliation, but only if you're willing to hit the restart button with Him and say no to your sin.

What happened to chivalry?

A woman longs to feel special, but a man longs to feel significant. He longs to feel strong and powerful, while a woman longs to feel beautiful and beyond compare. In chapter 2, the Shulamite called Solomon a stag twice in the same chapter, acknowledging him as a man of strength and power. He has called her an exceptional flower among all the thousands of flowers.

This primal need in both men and women goes all the way back to Genesis 1 and 2. When God created man and woman, He gave Adam dominion over the earth. God told him to subdue it, work it, and guard it. Adam was built for battle because he would ultimately battle both sin and Satan for dominion. God was charging Adam to not only tend the garden but to protect it. That is why in the heart of every man is the desire to be a protector, a provider, and somebody's knight in shining armor.

We live in an age when chivalry seems outdated and shunned as something demeaning to women. Wife, this does not mean you are so helpless that you need a man to save you. You may not need saving, but your husband wants to be your hero. Now that you know what is in his heart, you can begin to affirm that strength and conquering energy that is so deeply embedded in his male DNA. When my daughter was little, she never once asked me, "Daddy, do you want to wrestle?" When I would come home, it was, "Daddy, will you dance with me? Daddy, will you go on a date with me?"

On the other hand, almost every day, my boys would say, "Dad, let's wrestle. Dad, feel my muscles." As little boys, they wanted me to affirm their strength. Other times, they would say, "Dad, Dad, let me hit your chest." For them, Dad was the standard of strength. Nobody was stronger than Dad. When they wanted to wrestle, they were testing their strength against mine.

My sons are adults now. For many years, we went camping and canoeing every summer, and one of my sons always wanted to have a dunking contest with me. He finally got me—once out of 100 times, and he celebrated it. "Dad, I got you! Come on! Want a shot at the title? Come on. Let's do it again." That may sound silly, but it is a window into the heart of a man versus the heart of a woman. Not one time did my daughter ever want to dunk her dad.

My point is that as hard as the world tries to make men like women and women like men, we will never be the same. The failure to recognize we're not completely the same is the source of pain and frustration in marriage. Wives, remember that your husband fell in love with you not merely because of what you look like but because of what you made him feel like—a man. You made him feel good about his masculinity. He stays in love with you because you continue to make him feel strong and significant.

Husband, remember your wife fell in love with you—not because of what you looked like, but because of how you made her feel. You made her feel beautiful. You hear about people falling out of love all the time, and it's often because they quit doing the things that made them fall in love. He quit making her feel beautiful and special. She quit making him feel strong and powerful.

The way you stay in love is the same way you fell in love—with affection and admiration.

> *Nevertheless let each one of you in particular so love his own wife as himself, and let the wife see that she respects her husband* (Ephesians 5:33).

In this verse, the apostle Paul is recognizing the deepest needs of men and women in marriage. It's not that a man doesn't need his wife's love, but what he longs for is her respect. It's not that a wife doesn't need her husband's respect, but what she longs for is his love. I call this the "admiration-affection cycle" in marriage. It can work for you or against you.

There is a reason why nowhere in Scripture does God ever tell the man to respect his wife; and conversely, the wife is never commanded to love her husband. God will never tell you to do something you are naturally going to do. *Love comes naturally to women. Respect comes naturally to men.* Paul is telling us that the desires of a man's heart work in perfect harmony with the desires of a woman's heart. They work together, in tandem, in a way that brings beauty and unity and will grow their love and intimacy.

As the wife gives her husband admiration, it makes him have a deeper affection for his wife. As he gives affection to her, she naturally feels more admiration for him. This is the "give and receive" cycle of admiration and affection that God wants you to put in motion to help your love grow. It is not only how you fall in love, but how you stay in love.

When a wife withholds admiration or a husband withholds affection, that cycle begins working against them. When he withholds affection, she naturally feels less admiration. Because she starts withholding admiration, he naturally feels

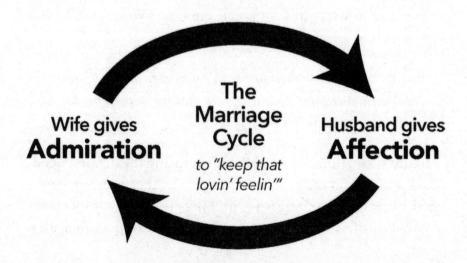

Wife gives **Admiration**

The Marriage Cycle to "keep that lovin' feelin'"

Husband gives **Affection**

less affection. And so the cycle goes—sometimes month after month, year after year.

Emotional Bank Accounts

They married with their emotional bank accounts full. They made many emotional deposits into each other's accounts, which is why they fell in love. However, once they were married, it became one withdrawal after another. Neither of them felt the admiration or affection they needed, and their emotional accounts were overdrawn. It may take years, but eventually, they will realize they are both emotionally bankrupt.

What do you do if this is you? You must reverse the cycle by once again making intentional deposits, putting it back in motion *for* you instead of it working *against* you. That is when you find yourselves in the beautiful rhythm of marriage.

How can you keep the admiration and affection rhythm of your marriage strong?

First and foremost, love your wife unconditionally. There are certainly times when none of us are especially lovable. Our wives are precious, but they, too, will have their moments. In the same way that God's unconditional love has the power to change us, a husband's unconditional love for his wife has the power to change her.

But God demonstrates His own love toward us, in that while we were still sinners, Christ died for us (Romans 5:8).

God didn't wait for us to become lovable to love us. He loved us when we weren't lovable, and it's His love that changes us. Love your wife like God loves you. Keep loving your wife, even when she is not lovable; and sooner or later, she will become more lovable.

When a man makes his wife feel beautiful, she will become more beautiful. When a man makes his wife feel treasured, she will act like a true treasure. Her husband is her mirror, and she will become what she sees when she looks into his eyes. Treat her like a queen, and she will become one.

You also need to compliment her openly. Don't wait for her to say, "How do I look in this dress?" What she is really asking is, "Do you still see me? Can I still capture your attention? Mirror, mirror on the wall, am I still beautiful to you at all?" Compliment her often and do it in front of others. Tell your wife often that you love her and that she is beautiful and special. While both men and women are visually driven, men are generally more visual, and women are generally more verbal. Your verbal affirmation is of immense importance.

Next, you should cover her with affection. That means physical affection that does not automatically lead to sex. Husband, you cannot skip the warm-ups to get to the main event. If you do, there will be no main event. Sometimes what you think is the warm-up is her main event.

Holding her hand, hugging, cuddling, and putting your arm around her are the non-sexual touches of affection that make her feel beautiful and special. Hold her hand in public. Put your arm around her when you go for a walk together. Hug her when you see her at the end of a long day. There are exceptions, of course, depending on our families of origin and how affectionate they were when we were growing up, but most women require more affection than men. It's what makes them feel truly loved and not just something desirable when we turn out the lights.

Lastly, create special memories. Your wife needs romance and passion more than once a year on Valentine's Day. You romanced her before you were married, so why have you stopped now that you're married? It doesn't have to cost much. Spend a few hours on a Saturday when it's just the two of you. Ask her what she would like to do. Maybe go for a walk at a nearby park or shopping at the local mall. Go sightseeing around your city. Take a drive through the country. Occasionally spend some money on your bride and plan a special weekend away. Life is busy, but women experience intimacy through quality time and communication.

Wife, here is how you can reach into the heart of your husband and meet his emotional needs. First, respect him unconditionally. God gives an unconditional command to husbands to *"love your wife as Christ loved the church."* Ephesians 5:33 is an unconditional command for wives to respect their husbands. The only question is, will you? You may think respect has to be earned. Well, yes and no.

> **While some respect must be earned, it must also be given.**

Even when you can't respect your husband for his actions, show him respect for his position as your husband. Just like love has the power to make your husband more lovable, respect has the power to make him more respectable. If you respect him even when he is not respectable, he will become a man who is more respectable and admirable.

A husband longs to be admired by his wife. Even when he isn't acting admirably, look for ways to show him admiration, and it will eventually make him more admirable. However, if he is continuously scorned like he is being reprimanded by his mother, his affection bank account will dry up. When that happens, your admiration account dries up as well. Respect him unconditionally in the same manner that God's Word says he is to love you unconditionally.

Next, it's important to encourage the conquering energy within him. When he goes fishing and is so excited because he caught the biggest fish of his life, a wise wife cares and says, "Honey, that is amazing. Let me take your picture!" He shoots his best game of golf ever, and he cannot wait to tell you all about it. "Honey, I shot 109." "Darling, I'm so proud of you!" (You know shooting a 109 isn't good, but that's not the point.) You are encouraging the conquering energy God put in him.

Men also need their strengths affirmed. Just like you need him to affirm your beauty, he needs you to affirm his strength. Sure, he has weaknesses, but he also has strengths that God created him with. There are things that he is good at, and he longs to know that you admire him and are proud of him.

Perhaps he's not great around the house. Something always needs to be repaired, and he's no Mr. Fixer-Upper. However, he works hard for a living and is a good provider for the family. Compliment him and show him appreciation. So he's not super athletic, but he is a talented artist. Compliment him and show him admiration. You wish he was more talkative and more intentional in your time together, but he is a great father and spends time in the backyard with the kids. You can nag him for what he doesn't do well or cheer him on for the things he does well. Cheering him on will take you both further.

Second, respond sexually to him. Many women may think sex is purely physical for a man, but it's not. It's how he connects intimately on an emotional level. I'll have more to say about this in the coming chapters, but for now, understand that men are the thermostat in the marriage, and women are the thermometers. Husbands set the temperature as far as how hot or cold it will be, and wives tell us how it really is. Men tend to think it is hotter in the marriage than it is; because we are the thermostat, we have the controls.

I want to encourage every married man to make the decision to become the greatest lover ever. I don't just mean in the bedroom. I mean in the living room as well because that's where love really begins. Do it, and you will put the sizzle back in your marriage instead of the fizzle.

— 7 —

MORE THAN MEETS
THE EYE

We have now come to Song of Solomon chapter 3, where our lovebirds finally tie the knot. God created marriage for more than any of us can imagine. Many people think marriage is about companionship. Yes, it is. A real marriage is about falling in love and experiencing the joy of intimacy. It's also about having a family, making babies, sex, and romance. Marriage is all those things and so much more.

To God, marriage is a picture of Christ's love for His bride and the gospel message that Jesus died for His bride to give her life. The greatest love story is what Jesus did on Calvary for all of humanity. God calls us His children. Anyone who has had a toddler around the house knows that before they can read, they learn by looking at pictures. It is the law of compare and contrast. This is what God does through His Word. The Bible is God's picture book.

When it comes to marriage, God presents picture after picture to help us understand our relationship with Jesus as the Bridegroom with His bride, the Church. God the Father builds on that picture in Ephesians 5, telling us that the physical union of a man and a woman in marriage portrays how husbands are a picture of Christ, and wives are a picture of the Church. Song of Solomon is another layer on that same picture to bring home our relationship with Him as well as our relationship with each other.

We are now at the point in Song of Solomon when the first stage of the Hebrew wedding begins. In Solomon's time, when the bridegroom saw a young lady whom he wanted to marry, he would approach her father about his intentions. They would come to terms and agree on the price—or dowry—of the bride. The more the young man was willing to pay, the greater the value he placed on her, and the greater honor it was for her.

A woman who was not married in Solomon's day was destined for poverty. Part of the dowry the father of the bride received was set aside in the event her husband died and she was left alone. This would ensure she wouldn't be destitute. This covenant mirrors the covenant God signed by the blood of His only begotten Son.

Remember, as the Church, we are in that same covenant stage of betrothal to Christ. I want to provide a deeper understanding of what it means to be the *bride of Christ.* Jesus gave us the new covenant the moment He declared with His dying breath on the Cross, "It is finished." It is only when you understand the imagery of the Hebrew wedding that you can really understand what Jesus accomplished for us when He shed His sinless blood on Calvary. When you begin to understand that He died to redeem the price of His fallen bride, His words take on a much deeper, prophetic meaning.

Communion Covenant

On the night before Jesus died, He instituted what we commonly call "communion" at the Last Supper. In some Christian traditions, we call this the Lord's Supper. When He and His disciples drank from a cup of wine, it became a memorial to Jesus' coming sacrifice on the Cross.

Remember, the Ketubah was signed by both the bridegroom and the father of the bride. This binding document specified both the price of the bride and the assurances the bridegroom was making to the bride to take care of her. For you and me, the bride of Christ, our Ketubah is the New Covenant—the New Testament—signed by the blood of Christ.

As part of this formal betrothal ceremony, the bridegroom would pour a cup of wine and offer it to his bride-to-be. With it, he was officially proposing to her and asking, "Will you marry me?" If she received the cup and drank from it, she was saying, "Yes, I do." If she refused to drink from the cup, she was saying "No way, José. Keep looking."

You can imagine how the bridegroom was on pins and needles as he poured her cup of wine, saying, "Will you receive the covenant? I want to be in a covenant relationship with you. I want to be betrothed to you." It is the very same thing Jesus did on the night before He died.

> *Then He took the cup, and gave thanks, and gave it to them, saying, "Drink from it, all of you. For this is My blood of the new covenant, which is shed for many for the remission of sins"* (Matthew 26:27-28).

Mirroring the Ketubah ceremony, Jesus was saying when He poured that cup of wine, "This wine is a picture of the blood of the new covenant. I'm about to shed My blood as the price for My bride." When His disciples received that cup, they were entering into a covenant with Him. Every time you take communion and drink from that cup, you say, "I'm in covenant with Jesus as my Bridegroom. I accept the terms of the Ketubah."

From the day her bridegroom left to prepare their bridal chamber, the Shulamite bride was preparing herself only for him. She would have daily beauty treatments and perfume baths. She had no idea when he was coming back; she just knew he was coming. She had to be ready every day for her bridegroom to return to carry her back to his father's house to consummate their marriage. This is what Jesus has planned for every born-again Christian. One day, He is going to come for His bride—the Church of the Lord Jesus Christ. That is why the apostle Paul writes in 2 Corinthians 11:2:

> *For I am jealous for you with godly jealousy. For I have betrothed you to one husband, that I may present you as a chaste virgin to Christ.*

God is showing us the heart of the Bridegroom. As the Church of Jesus Christ, we are charged with keeping ourselves solely for Him and not giving in to sin.

We don't know how long, but perhaps even months have gone by between chapters 2 and 3. Solomon went back to Jerusalem to prepare a bridal chamber for his bride, as was customary for every Jewish wedding. As our Jewish Bridegroom, Jesus has gone to His Father's house to prepare a bridal chamber for His bride. One day soon He will return to carry her back to His Father's house as He promised in John 14:1-6. Like Solomon's bride-to-be, we don't know for sure when our Bridegroom will return for us. But we have the promise of His Word which is enough. Our job as the bride is to be radiant and ready.

Anxiety, Insecurity, and Dreams

Like the bride of Christ, the Shulamite had no idea when Solomon would come back for her. She lived in the area far to the north of Jerusalem where Solomon had gone. He was away for a long time, and she began to get insecure, thinking he might not come back at all. She was plagued with a recurring dream. It was a bad dream that revealed her anxiety.

> *By night on my bed I sought the one I love; I sought him, but I did not find him. "I will rise now," I said, "and go about the city; in the streets and in the squares I will seek the one I love." I sought him, but I did not find him. The watchmen who go about the city found me; I said, "Have you seen the one I love?" Scarcely had I passed by them, when I found the one I love. I held him and would not let him go, until I had brought him to the house of my mother, and into the chamber of her who conceived me* (Song of Solomon 3:1-4).

This passage gives us tremendous insight into this young bride-to-be. Our dreams often reveal our insecurities. When I was a part of the Kansas City Police Department, I had a recurring dream about pulling over a Camaro convertible full of bad guys. The top was down on the convertible with two people in the front seat and two in the back. As I approached the car, the driver got the drop on me. In a flash, he turned around with a smile on his face and pointed his 44 Magnum stainless steel handgun at my chest. It went off with a loud bang, and that is when I woke up. I had that dream multiple times. In law enforcement, we commonly call that a cop dream.

Many years ago, I also had a preacher dream. I had this dream on more than one occasion. Once a year, we had a church picnic at one of the local lakes, where we also baptized people. In my dream, hundreds of people were everywhere. Suddenly, everybody looked at me, and women were putting their hands over their mouths and men had their hands over their eyes. I looked down to see that I was in my underwear. I thought to myself, *What am I doing in my underwear? How can I get out of here?* Fortunately, I haven't had that dream for a long while.

The Shulamite also had a dream that revealed her insecurity. She feared Solomon didn't really love her or that he might not come back for her. Her dream was about a lost love. She is a picture of all of us, just as Solomon is a picture of Jesus. It reflects another bride who ate of a certain tree, and paradise was lost. Like the Shulamite's dream, we all have a love that we lost.

Where there is sin, there is always separation.

The Shulamite had not kept her sexual purity, and she was ostracized by her family. We have all become fallen brides. Because of Eve, we have all eaten from that tree.

> *All have sinned and fall short of the glory of God* (Romans 3:23).

The moment Adam and Eve ate from the fruit of the tree in the Garden, they were separated from God. Their eyes were opened, and they realized what they had done. Their first response to their sin was to sew fig leaves together to cover up their nakedness and shame. The Shulamite is a picture of us because she is a picture of Eve. We were all in Eve in Genesis chapter 3. She is the mother of us all. When she ate, we all ate. Consequently, sin is the reason for insecurity.

We all have insecurities, regardless of how confident, polished, or put together we may seem. The insecurity stems from our sin. We were born with brokenness and baggage. Why? Because we all fell under Adam's condemnation because we were *in* Adam. The moment Adam took a bite of that fruit, he died, and we died with him.

While man is into cover-ups, Jesus is into clean-ups.

The fig leaves are what we choose to cover up who we are. The reason intimacy is so difficult in marriage is because of our insecurities. We all come into our marriages as fallen daughters of Eve and fallen sons of Adam. We wear fig leaves because of sin committed by us or sin committed against us. We must end the cover-up if we are going to have true intimacy in marriage.

Remember, *intimacy* means "in-to-me-see." Intimacy happens when there is such security relationally that we let someone see into us, with all of our hitches and hangups, anxieties and insecurities, faults and flaws. Yet we are secure enough in each other's love that we can be truly "naked and not ashamed" (Genesis 2:25) like Adam and Eve were before they sinned.

Insecurity is the enemy of intimacy.

Solomon's bride-to-be is insecure because of her past actions and the way her brothers made her work in the sun. She wore the stigma of her sin on her skin for the whole world to see. She was not happy with what she did, but she met this wonderful shepherd king who came to redeem her and pay a high price for her. Now he is away, and it has been a while since she has seen him.

Her story is our story. The only way to truly get past your insecurities so you can really enjoy marital intimacy is to come into a personal relationship with Jesus, not another person. Jesus brings about the clean-up, so you don't have to go through life with the cover-up. Only when you are secure in His love can you ever feel truly secure in the love of another.

This is the meaning of 1 John 4:18: *"There is no fear in love; but perfect love casts out fear...."*

Only Jesus can love you perfectly. He knows everything about you but loves you unconditionally. There is no reason to keep hiding in fear and shame. Only when you know you are loved perfectly can you have the security to foster the deepest levels of marital intimacy. When you no longer have anything to hide from God, you need not hide anything from each other.

This young woman lay in her bed and told us about her dream of a love that was lost and the hope that she could find him. One day she saw her king coming, just like he said he would. He came and received her unto himself so that where he is, there she may also be (John 14:3).

> *Who is this coming out of the wilderness like pillars of smoke, perfumed with myrrh and frankincense, with all the merchant's fragrant powders? Behold, it is Solomon's couch, with sixty valiant men around it, of the valiant of Israel. They all hold swords, being expert in war. Every man has his sword on his thigh because of fear in the night* (Song of Solomon 3:6-8).

She saw Solomon coming in a cloud of dust from his entourage that accompanied him with great pomp and ceremony—just like Jesus has promised to one day return in a "cloud" with an angelic host accompanying Him (Acts 1:9-11). This was a beautiful picture pointing to the day when Jesus returns for us, His bride. He is the Jewish Bridegroom who promised one day to take us back to His Father's house where He is preparing a place for you and me, His Church.

Interestingly, she saw Solomon coming "perfumed with myrrh and frankincense"—the identical ointments that anointed our Savior's body when He laid down His life for His bride. Solomon's 60 bodyguards, made up of the palace guard, are carrying him to retrieve the love of his life on an elaborate couch with a covering on top of it. It's called a palanquin, and he will use it to carry her back to Jerusalem in style. Verses 9-10 describe the opulence of Solomon's palanquin and how he directed the construction of every detail:

> *Of the wood of Lebanon Solomon the King made himself a palanquin: He made its pillars of silver, its support of gold, its seat of purple, its interior paved with love by the daughters of Jerusalem.*

Only God could create such masterful imagery and parallels. In chapter 1 when Solomon comes for the Shulamite, he is introduced as a shepherd. In chapter 3, he comes as a king. Why? Because this is a picture of the first and second coming of Christ. The first time Jesus came as a Shepherd.

> *I am the good shepherd. The good shepherd gives His life for the sheep* (John 10:11).

The second time, He is not coming as a shepherd but as the King. The first time He came to suffer, but the second time He is coming back to conquer. The first time He came for a cross, but the second time He is coming for a crown. When He does, He is going to carry the bride He has redeemed back to His Father's house. The last thing the Shulamite would have heard Solomon say as he went back to Jerusalem are the same words Jesus spoke as a Jewish Bridegroom on the night before His death:

> *Let not your heart be troubled; you believe in God, believe also in Me. In My Father's house are many mansions; if it were not so, I would have told you. I go to prepare a place for you. And if I go and prepare a place for you, I will come again and*

receive you to Myself; that where I am, there you may be also (John 14:1-3).

Solomon went back to prepare a bridal chamber in his father's house. When it was complete, he returned, as promised, for his bride. For the past 2,000 years, our Bridegroom, the Lord Jesus Christ, has been in His Father's house, preparing a room for us. The entire ancient Hebrew wedding process is a picture of what Jesus will do when He returns for His bride, the Church, and carries us back to Heaven.

> *For the Lord Himself will descend from heaven with a shout, with the voice of an archangel, and with the trumpet of God. And the dead in Christ will rise first. Then we who are alive and remain shall be caught up together with them in the clouds to meet the Lord in the air. And thus we shall always be with the Lord* (1 Thessalonians 4:16-17).

Jesus has prepared a place for you, and there is coming a day when He is going to return for His bride. We don't know when it will be, but I'm convinced He is coming much sooner than many think or believe. I truly believe we are living on the very threshold of our Savior's return. As the bride, we need to be rapture-ready! Biblically and prophetically, there's not one thing that remains unfulfilled that would keep Jesus from returning for His bride at this very moment.

Song of Solomon foreshadows the return of Jesus, as He and His bride are carried by the strong arms of these mighty men. It is a vivid picture of the Rapture when they will then consummate their marriage in the bridal chamber He has prepared. Revelation 19 tells us that just as the ancient Hebrews had a seven-day wedding feast, so we will be wed to Jesus, our Bridegroom, at the seven-day wedding feast in Heaven, while the world endures seven years of tribulation. You simply cannot understand everything you are to Jesus and how much you matter to Him until you are able to see the big picture of marriage.

There is more to marriage than meets the eye.

Men, if you want to be a great bridegroom, you must learn how to be a great bride—a follower of Jesus Christ. I realize it's hard for most of us as men to get our minds around being a bride—even if it's the bride of Christ. The imagery is meant first to teach us about our relationship with Jesus; and second, to teach us how to embody His love for us in how we love our wives.

Remember, whether you are married or not, you are already loved perfectly and completely. No one will ever love you more than Jesus who loves you passionately and unconditionally, without end. Only when you understand deep down in your spirit that you are already loved perfectly can you love another in the same way. God's love is a selfless love.

Human love takes; God's love gives.

Marriages often become parasitic. He is trying to take from her, and she is trying to take from him. They are just two broken people, full of insecurities, trying to *get* life from each other, but they only end up *taking* life from each other. Life can only come from God—not our spouse.

By loving like Christ, we lay down our lives for each other, thereby giving life to one another. Marriages die when two people act like they're still alive. When two people have died to themselves, they give life to each other; and in doing so, they give life to their marriage. Like Jesus' love for us, this demands a cross—the one on which we die. The day you said, "I do" is the day you said, "I die." Only then can your marriage live.

Once you realize you are loved perfectly by Christ, you are okay if occasionally your spouse fails to love you perfectly. Honestly, this will happen more than occasionally. That is when you embrace the Cross required in marriage. You willingly take the nails. Your spouse is only human after all, and they are going to have some bad moments and even bad days along the way. They are not going to love you perfectly every day. Only Jesus can love you that way.

Because you are loved that way by Christ, you can give that love away by practicing 1 Peter 4:8, which says, *"And above all things have fervent love for one another, for 'love will cover a multitude of sins.'"* Love does not cover up sin and look the other way; love covers sin. Love calls it what it is and then says, "I'll give you the grace and forgiveness needed to cover your sin." That's what Jesus did for us, and that's what we do for each other in marriage. Grace and forgiveness are constantly being given and received.

To Complement, Not Complete

Remember, your spouse is not meant to complete you, only complement you. That is where so much of the dysfunction in marriage begins. Adam was created in the express image and likeness of God. It does not get more complete than that. Adam was not incomplete because he was single. Adam was complete because he was made in the image and likeness of God.

As a born-again child of God, you, too, now bear the image of God. You are as complete as you will ever be in Him. Only when you realize you are complete in Christ already, can you have a marriage where two people truly complement each other rather than compete with each other. Competing fosters codependency and parasitic relationships that are so common in marriage.

That is why so many marriages are full of endless strife. It's because we let Hollywood and romantic comedies shape what we think about love and romance and marriage, instead of God. There is a very famous line from the movie *Jerry McGuire,* played by Hollywood heartthrob Tom Cruise. He looks at his lover and says, "I love you...you complete me." It's very dramatic and moving. It will make your heart melt. The problem is that it's only true in the movies. It's not true in real life.

> No one can complete you but the One who made you.

No one can complete you but the One who made you. This is why Hollywood romance movies always end with the couple finally declaring their love for each other. They might even show the wedding and end the movie with the couple locked arm in arm at the reception. Hooray for another happy ending. But that's not the ending. It's only the beginning. Have you noticed they rarely make any movies about what happens after the wedding? They love to tell the story of people falling in love, but seldom do they tell the story of people staying in love.

Many people naturally accept the view of pop culture that we complete each other when we get married. The reason they often begin to compete with each other is because they married someone just like them—another incomplete, broken, sinful person. Their marriage has become a parasitic relationship, constantly sucking life from each other instead of giving life to one another.

When we stop asking another human being to do things human beings were never meant to do, we can begin to get the honey back after the honeymoon.

Sanctification and Satisfaction

To God, your marriage is more for your sanctification than for your satisfaction. Sanctification is the process of being conformed to the image of Jesus Christ (Romans 8:29). As Christians, God's plan for us is to become like Christ. Marriage is one of God's tools to complete that process in us—not simply for our own gratification. Marriage is for His glorification. In marriage, we learn how to love unconditionally and give mercy. In marriage, we learn how to give grace and forgiveness. We learn what it means to love like Christ loves the Church. If we pursue our marriage as though it is for our sanctification, we will discover satisfaction.

If we try to be satisfied apart from being sanctified, we will never be sanctified nor satisfied.

The reason there is so much marital dissatisfaction is because we think it's all about us when it's supposed to be all about Jesus. The next time your spouse hurts your feelings and you want to retaliate, try having a little talk with your Savior first. "Jesus, I know this is a tool right now to make me more like You, so help me not to retaliate with anger. Help me to respond with kindness and forgiveness." Suddenly you will find yourself giving grace instead of retribution. You'll be amazed at what it will do for both of you.

Marriage is more than meets the eye. It is meant to draw a picture of the Holy Trinity. God is one God, eternally existing in three Persons—Father, Son, and Holy Spirit. Not three gods but three Persons within the Godhead. Marriage is meant to be a man and a woman in perfect harmony with God, the Father.

> *For the husband is head of the wife, as also Christ is head of the church; and He is the Savior of the body. Therefore, just as the church is subject to Christ, so let the wives be to their own husbands in everything* (Ephesians 5:23-24).

The husband is the head of the wife because he's a picture of Christ. I know we live in a society where many women take issue with this passage, but it's because they don't understand what it means. They've been lied to about what it means for the husband to be the head of the wife. They've been taught it's archaic and misogynistic. Let me be clear. The fact that Scripture teaches the man is the head of the wife does not imply he's supposed to be her boss and she is just some poor subservient underling waiting to jump at whatever he commands.

The husband is the head because he is a picture of Christ, who died for His bride (Ephesians 5:25). What woman wouldn't love to be married to a man like that? The fact that the man is the head makes him the leader in the same sense that Jesus leads us. Paul is obviously not talking about just any husband but a husband who is following Jesus and is a picture of our Savior. Remember, marriage is meant to draw a picture of the Holy Trinity. As husbands and wives, we are in unity with God the Father. The husband is a picture of God the Son, and the wife is a picture of God the Spirit.

Genesis 2:18 tells us, "*The Lord God said, 'It is not good that man should be alone; I will make him a helper comparable to him.'*" God was about to bring Adam a bride from Adam's side. He would describe her as a "helper"—the very same title Jesus attributed to the Holy Spirit (John 14:26).

Ladies, your husband represents the Son, and you represent the Spirit. *Your husband is the head of the home, but you are the heart of the home.* Both the head and the heart are indispensable to the plans and purposes of God. Both the Son of God and the Spirit of God are co-equal members of the Trinity in union with the Father. It's time to end the battle of the sexes forever. We are all equal parts, though we differ in function.

Now let's take this picture even further. The apostle Paul teaches in Ephesians 5:22-32 that marriage is a picture of our relationship to Jesus as a bride to a Bridegroom. But we are more than the bride of Christ. The New Testament also calls the Church the *body* of Christ.

> *For we are members of His body, of His flesh and of His bones. "For this reason a man shall leave his father and mother and be joined to his wife, and the two shall become one flesh"* (Ephesians 5:30-31).

God desires that a husband and wife be joined together into one flesh, as in one person. This is why Paul writes in Ephesians 5:28, *"So husbands ought to love their own wives as their own bodies...."* If the two are now "one flesh" and the husband is the head, then his bride is his body, as the Church is the bride and body of the Lord Jesus Christ.

So in marriage, who is the more important partner, the husband or wife? That's like trying to answer which is more important to your person—your head or your body? The truth is neither can survive without the other. Ephesians 5:21 says, *"submitting to one another in the fear of God."* The body submits to the lead of the head while the head submits to the needs of the body. His lead. Her need.

Unity with Him means intimacy with each other.

When both husband and wife are growing spiritually in unity, you will experience the deepest intimacy known in marriage. You will increasingly become one flesh. When the two of you are growing personally in your relationship with the Father, you are growing in your relationship with each other as well. Everything flows out of your relationship with God. Unity with Him means intimacy with each other.

---8---

SACRED AND SIZZLING SEX

I understand that sex can be an extremely sensitive subject for many people who have been hurt by it. Everything that God means for good, Satan attempts to use for evil. We live in a sexualized culture that wants to tear apart the boundaries that God has put around this area of our lives. God does not put boundaries in our lives to oppress us but to protect us. Society has erased those lines. The result is a culture that is producing sexual predators, perverts, and prisoners. Sexual abuse is on the rise, and no doubt many who are reading this book have been affected by this very thing. Satan has stolen and corrupted something very precious that God wants to give us.

My prayer is that you will grow in everything God wants to do in and through you. For some, it's time to take something back that Satan stole from you because it belongs to you as a child of God. It's sacred ground, and too much of the time, church culture has refused to talk about it. Consequently, our fallen, sinful world has succeeded in framing the conversation around sex and ignoring all that God's Word has to say about it.

Song of Solomon chapter 4 begins in the bridal chamber where God invites us into the couple's honeymoon night. It's their first night together as a married couple. Solomon returned for his bride and carried her back to Jerusalem to his father's house where they began their seven-day wedding feast. The *consummation* is the second stage of the ancient Hebrew wedding.

While God views sex as something sacred, society's view is the exact opposite—it's seen as merely a "sandbox" for grownups to play in. In fact, we might call our modern society's view of sex the pornographer's view of sex or the promiscuous view that says sex is primarily for our personal gratification. This view says it's okay to have sex with whomever you want, whenever you want, however you want, and abandon limits as long as it involves two consenting individuals.

Our increasingly toxic culture says God's views are outdated; we're now an "enlightened" society. I would suggest the data reveals we are descending into darkness. We've erased the lines of biblical morality. Consequently, we're paying a dire penalty. America now has the highest rates in the history of our nation of addiction, depression, suicide, and STDs among teenagers.

While we denounce sex trafficking and the objectification of women, we simultaneously seek to sexualize our children at younger and younger ages. The pornography industry and social media platforms have created an incubator for sexual perverts, predators, and prisoners.

We've sown to the wind, and we are reaping a whirlwind.

There's another view that's just as unbiblical as the pornographer's view that I call *the Puritan view.* If you were raised in church, there is a good chance you were raised with this view of sex. The Puritans were the Pilgrims who landed on Plymouth Rock. They were very devout, religious people with an extremely legalistic and unbiblical view of sex. They viewed it as only for procreation and not to be enjoyed. It was generally something to be avoided. It was considered dirty and seen as a necessary evil for the sole purpose of reproduction.

This distorted view of sex shaped the views of many American Christians in varying degrees over the course of generations. Sex in many Christian homes has been seen as taboo. And if you must say the word "sex," it's in hushed tones and whispers. It is something we "just don't talk about." The problem with refusing to talk about it is that we are teaching the next generation it must be dirty. Just like the pornographer's view, this could not be further from the truth, though both views are at opposite ends of the spectrum. In the eyes of God, sex is not only sacred—it is to be celebrated. We see this throughout Scripture.

> *Marriage is honorable among all, and the bed undefiled; but fornicators and adulterers God will judge* (Hebrews 13:4).

The author of Hebrews was saying that it's not sinful to have sizzling sex in marriage. God did not create it just to make a baby. God made it pleasurable to bless you. You are not going to defile anything in the marriage bed in the eyes of God. He has blessed it, but He also says in that same verse that if we choose to cross God's boundaries in our lives, there will be a penalty. Fornication means any sexual activity outside of marriage. God will not bless sin. He must judge it.

Consequently, we live in a society that is increasingly under judgment, going further and further into depravity and moral anarchy. Moral anarchy is captivity and slavery, and tragically, this is where many find themselves.

Many have been hurt by sex because somebody crossed the line. Sin was either inflicted on us or by us. All sin leaves a scar, but always remember that Jesus is the Healer. It is the reason He came.

But He was wounded for our transgressions, He was bruised for our iniquities; the chastisement for our peace was upon Him, and by His stripes we are healed (Isaiah 53:5).

Regardless of where you've been or what you've done, Jesus brings about a resurrection to what has died. He restores what has been lost, He rebuilds what has broken, and He wants to do it in your life. Not only is sex sacred, but God created it to sizzle. Far too many in society believe the only great sex is extramarital or premarital sex. You may be thinking that married sex is so predictable that it must be boring, but that couldn't be further from the truth.

In Song of Solomon chapter 4, the newlyweds have gone into the bridal chamber to consummate their marriage, where things start to really heat up. Beginning in verse 1, Solomon slowly undresses his wife from the top down. He removes the veil first and then takes down her hair so it falls over her shoulders. She is showing her teeth, and he compliments her beautiful smile. The metaphors he uses to describe her beauty are certain to make us smile, if not outright laugh.

Behold, you are fair, my love! Behold, you are fair! You have dove's eyes behind your veil. Your hair is like a flock of goats, going down from Mount Gilead. Your teeth are like a flock of shorn sheep which have come up from the washing, every one of which bears twins, and none is barren among them. Your lips are like a strand of scarlet, and your mouth is lovely. Your temples behind your veil are like a piece of pomegranate. Your neck is like the tower of David, built for an armory, on which hang a thousand bucklers, all shields of mighty men. Your two breasts are like two fawns, twins of a gazelle, which feed among the lilies. Until the day breaks and the shadows flee away, I will go my way to the

mountain of myrrh and to the hill of frankincense (Song
of Solomon 4:1-6).

Fortunately for Solomon, none of his bride's teeth are barren. She has them all. *"Like a flock of shorn sheep coming up from
the washing."* Apparently, they are nice and white too! She is
smiling because she is happy to be with him. He is drawn to
her beautiful teeth and her mouth in verse 3. The mouth has
always been a sensual part of a woman's body, which is why
women have painted their lips for eons.

In verse 4, he describes the beautiful necklace around her
neck. A woman wears jewelry because it makes her feel beautiful, and he is responding to that beauty. In verse 5, Solomon
is now taking off her dress. For the first time, he sees her two
breasts, describing them as two fawns and twins of gazelles.
Fawns are very gentle and skittish creatures.

Solomon is showing every newlywed husband how to behave
on their honeymoon night. Don't rip your shirt off like Conan
the Barbarian and come racing in to attack your wife. Move
slowly, gently, and carefully. You may be ready to move at the
speed of light, but a woman needs to warm up.

In verse 6, he continues to move down her body, and he is
enraptured by her love. Here is a woman who is now standing naked before her husband. Solomon says the words every
woman longs to hear—she is beautiful and without blemish in
the eyes of her husband.

Husband, if you want your wife to respond sexually, completely uninhibited, it is crucial that you help her know that
in a world of fantasy, virtual reality, airbrushed pictures, and
body images of fitness models, she is beautiful and perfect in
every way. A woman knows the places on her body that make
her insecure. A wise husband knows where they are as well and
removes all of her insecurity by complimenting her openly.

When we met the young maiden in chapter 1, she was very insecure about her appearance, specifically her sun-darkened skin. But all that insecurity is gone now in her husband's presence. While some men may look in the mirror and see a bodybuilder, women will often look in the mirror and see things they wish they could change about themselves.

But this woman is now standing completely naked and uninhibited before her husband because he made her feel beautiful and completely secure in his presence. This should be the goal of every husband—to create such safety and security relationally that our wives can be naked and not ashamed (Genesis 2:25).

That's exactly how Jesus sees every one of us. Remember, Solomon is a picture of Christ. Paul wrote in Ephesians 5:27 that in the eyes of Jesus, you are already without spot or blemish. He washed away every wrinkle by the blood He shed on Calvary and made you holy and perfect, without blame. Our wives lose all of their insecurity when they know we don't see their flaws. It is our responsibility to make sure they know they are perfect in our eyes.

This is a woman who is now absolutely secure in the presence of her husband. In Song of Solomon 4:8, she says, *"Come with me from Lebanon.... Look from the top of Amana, from the top of Senir and Hermon, from the lions' dens, from the mountains of the leopards."*

Lebanon was a wild, untamed territory to the north of Solomon's kingdom where lions and other wild beasts roamed. Some have suggested from this verse that perhaps the Shulamite was from Lebanon. It's possible since Solomon was, in fact, in alliance with the king of Lebanon. He most certainly had traveled there on multiple occasions. Others, however, speculate that she was from the town of Shunem of the tribe of Issachar in the northern region of Israel.

We don't know for sure, but either way, Solomon brought her back to Jerusalem—a place of safety and security. Solomon assures her that she is safe with him. Husbands have the responsibility of ensuring their wives have a complete sense of safety, devoid of insecurity and anxiety. She feels protected in his presence. For a woman to respond sexually, she must feel completely safe.

> *You have ravished my heart, my sister, my spouse; you have ravished my heart with one look of your eyes, with one link of your necklace. How fair is your love, my sister, my spouse! How much better than wine is your love, and the scent of your perfumes than all spices! Your lips, O my spouse, drip as the honeycomb; honey and milk are under your tongue; and the fragrance of your garments is like the fragrance of Lebanon. A garden enclosed is my sister, my spouse, a spring shut up, a fountain sealed. Your plants are an orchard of pomegranates with pleasant fruits, fragrant henna with spikenard, spikenard and saffron, calamus and cinnamon, with all trees of frankincense, myrrh and aloes, with all the chief spices—a fountain of gardens, a well of living waters, and streams from Lebanon* (Song of Solomon 4:9-15).

It is really heating up in their bridal chamber when even one link from her necklace is now enough to turn him on. The key to sex that sizzles is friendship and trust. Three times in this passage, Solomon calls her *"my sister, my spouse,"* in the same way in a Christian marriage, you are her brother, and she is your sister. My wife is my spouse, but she is also my sister in Christ. It implies friendship and trust. This is why the best sex is always going to be married sex. Sex outside of marriage will always leave you longing, and it will always fall short of God's intended best for your life. It takes time to build this deep trust and friendship.

Regardless of what the movies portray, you cannot really have the deepest, hottest sex with somebody you don't know—especially in our hook-up culture. It may be exciting and have a sense of intensity, but it is not intimacy. God created us with a longing for not merely intensity but intimacy. Solomon now knows this woman deeply. They are not only lovers—they are friends. Acknowledging that she is his sister and his spouse is the very foundation of sacred sex that truly sizzles. There is an understanding and knowledge there. There is familiarity, and with it comes intimacy.

"How much better than wine is your love, and the scent of your perfumes than all spices!" This is a man who is absolutely intoxicated with his wife. He considers her better than wine. The perfume that she wears is more potent than all the spices of the world. Up to this point, this couple has not even kissed.

Verse 11 records their first kiss on their honeymoon night. *"Your lips, oh my spouse, drip as the honeycomb. Honey and milk are under your tongue."* France didn't become a nation until around AD 900. But almost 1,900 years earlier, Solomon invented the French kiss, and they are making out hot and heavy.

In verse 12 he says, *"A garden enclosed is my sister, my spouse."* Her garden is her body and her sexuality. In those days, every family had a garden. They would build walls around it with a gate and locks to keep people from stealing from it and animals from destroying it.

Solomon affirms his bride's virtue. Their relationship is all about trust, and there is security on both sides. There is faithfulness, purity, and integrity with sacred sex that sizzles. This is a woman who has locked her garden to any man other than her husband.

He begins by describing the fruit and the taste of coming into this garden that he has nurtured and watered to pick the fruit of this garden. *"A garden enclosed is my sister, my spouse, a spring shut up, a fountain sealed.*" This couple is really getting turned on. *"Your plants are an orchard of pomegranates with pleasant fruits, fragrant henna with spikenard, spikenard and saffron, calamus and cinnamon, with all trees of frankincense, myrrh, and aloes, with all the chief spices—a fountain of gardens, a well of living waters, and streams from Lebanon."*

Verse 16 is the one time the bride speaks in this chapter: *"Awake, O north wind, and come, O south! Blow upon my garden, that its spices may flow out. Let my beloved come to his garden and eat its pleasant fruits."*

This man has turned her on, and the winds are starting to blow. Her world is starting to shake, and she is about to get carried away. At this point, God closes the curtain on this couple. He does not let us know what happens next because it is too sacred. He gives this couple their privacy.

> God wants us to enjoy everything He has given us as married couples.

The next time we hear from our lovebirds is in chapter 5:1 after they have consummated the marriage.

> *I have come to my garden, my sister, my spouse; I have gathered my myrrh with my spice; I have eaten my honeycomb with my honey; I have drunk my wine with my milk.*

While God inspired this entire Song, the Lord gave Himself just one line in the entire Song of Solomon. Song of Solomon chapter 5:1 says, *"Eat, O friends! Drink, yes, drink deeply, O beloved ones!"* God wants us to enjoy everything He has given us as married couples. God was not rebuking them and telling them they needed to repent because they had too much fun. At times, the Church has been part of the problem with a pornographic view of sex outside the Church and a puritanical view of sex within the Church. Yet here is the God of Heaven looking down on this married couple and blessing them. He wants them to enjoy the sweetest fruits of the garden He has given them.

Four Wishes

The following are *four things every man wishes his wife knew.* Knowing these four things will improve your sexual intimacy in marriage. Wife, listen carefully, and don't worry. I have a list for your husband as well.

Number One: Your husband wants you to know that his sex drive is powerful, persistent, and normal. Wife, if you have ever thought that your husband couldn't get enough, know that God made him that way. A man has ten times the amount of testosterone in his body than a woman has in her body. It's the sexual energy that drives his libido. He naturally will have a stronger sex drive than a woman; but in some marriages, the wife has the stronger sex drive. There are exceptions to almost everything. But generally, most husbands are more sexually driven than their brides.

Consequently, a lot of women think, *we just had sex a few days ago; it's not like he is going to die without it.* No, he won't die without it; he is just going to feel like it. There isn't something wrong with him. It is crucial as his wife that you understand this is how God made him. It is also vital that you understand that while he does consistently need a physical release, sex is more than just physical for him.

Number Two: Sex is how men bond with their wives emotionally and intimately. Most women understand that sex is physical for men, but they may not understand how deeply emotional it is as well.

A woman feels close to a man when they spend time talking together. In the same way, a woman won't feel intimate with a husband who ignores her and hasn't talked to her for days. A husband will feel the same way if his wife ignores him sexually.

Remember, Genesis 2:24 says a man shall leave his father and mother and cleave, or be joined, to his wife, and they shall be one flesh. *Joined* in Hebrew literally means to "bond or glue." The only time that oxytocin in a man's brain reaches the levels of a woman's brain is when he climaxes with his wife.

Thousands of years ago, the Bible records what couldn't have been comprehended scientifically but what we now know happens in the brain. Wife, you will feel distant if your husband doesn't talk to you for the next two weeks. It's the same for your husband if he hasn't had sex with you for two weeks.

There are several cycles God put in marriage that can work for or against us. I explained earlier the affection/admiration cycle. Another cycle is what happens when your husband deeply meets your emotional needs through quality time and talking. When he spends time talking to you, you naturally feel more intimate with him and are more ready to respond to him sexually. As you respond sexually to him, he starts to feel affection toward you and wants to spend time talking to you.

When that account starts to run dry, that same cycle starts to work against you. You find yourself withdrawing, and you begin to drift apart. When you stop responding sexually, he starts to run dry in affection, and before you know it, you are both in emotional bankruptcy. This is why it is so crucial that you understand what is really going on in the heart of a man and in your own heart as well.

Number Three: *Sizzling sex.* This kind of sex doesn't happen when you are just doing your duty as a Christian wife. Why does it matter so much to the average man? It reassures a man of his masculinity, and consequently, his thoughts and feelings hinge on it. Passionate sex makes him feel strong in every area of his life. It goes beyond the bedroom. Remember, a man's number one need is to feel strong and powerful about his masculinity. When a man doesn't feel good about his sexuality, he doesn't feel good about himself, and it affects every area of his life.

If a man feels impotent in bed, he feels impotent in every other area of his life too. Viagra commercials used to show a man walking through his office with a confident look on his face, and his coworkers said, "Hey, there's something different about you today. Did you get a haircut? Did you lose weight?" And the man didn't respond with anything more than a very contented smile.

The marketers understood what sex really is to a man. That man was confident because he had a great sex life. A lot of men can't make their women feel beautiful because they don't feel strong themselves. Great sex is one of the things that makes him feel strong. If he doesn't feel good about himself, he can't make you feel good about yourself. For a man to make a woman feel beautiful and special, he must feel like he is strong enough to do it. Otherwise, he will retreat from whatever area of his life makes him feel weak. Passionate sex reassures him of his masculinity and makes him feel desirable and lovable.

Number Four: *Real sexual fulfillment for a man is impossible if he cannot sexually fulfill his wife.* A lot of women understand the need to take care of their husbands. They think, "If I fulfill him and gratify him physically, he'll get the fix he needs." While he may get a fix temporarily, it will still leave him longing and empty. His number one desire is that he becomes your desire the way you are his desire. He wants you to want him in the same way he wants you.

Shaunti Feldhahn wrote a book called *For Women Only*. In it, she provides the results of several of her research surveys of men. One of the questions was, "If your wife offers all the sex you want but does it reluctantly or simply to accommodate your sexual needs, will you be sexually satisfied?" Seventy-four percent of men said, "No."

Getting all the sex men want is not really what they desire. They deeply need to satisfy you as well, or they are not truly satisfied. As Shaunti Feldhahn said, "As much as a man wants and needs sex, most men would rather clean the gutters in the freezing rain than have sex with a woman who acts like she's completely uninterested." If your attitude is to just get it over with, it may gratify him for the moment, but it leaves him empty when it's over.

If you are just going through the motions, not *there* in the moment, not trying to get *there* with him, it says that he is not enough of a man to satisfy you. If he can't turn you on no matter how hard he tries, his masculinity no longer feels good. For a man, sex can be risky because he is really putting his masculinity on the line.

God gave man an ego and conquering energy—the need to feel strong. When the male ego becomes egotistical or narcissistic, it is sinful. On the other hand, when a man is emasculated, he loses his swagger. He can no longer be the man God made him to be. Wife, you want your husband to have a little swag. This is part of that confidence that God gave men to feel good about being a man. If you come with the classic line, "I am too tired tonight," you may be too tired, but he hears, "You couldn't turn me on if your life depended on it. You can't even compete with a pillow."

Husband, at times, you need to let her roll over and go to sleep because she is genuinely tired. Die to your needs to live for her needs. Your sexual energy is fueled by testosterone, and her sexual energy is fueled by the same pool of energy that she used chasing the kids around all day or driving in rush hour traffic. She is exhausted. Give her a break, and do not take it personally. She is not rejecting you even though it may feel like it at the time.

It is not right to leverage sex against our wives or guilt them into it. Marriage is about dying to self to meet the needs of the other. Sometimes that is what wives need to do. You really are tired, but you are going to die to your need to meet his needs. You might tell him ahead of time that you are really exhausted and might not fully get there so he's not disappointed and knows ahead of time what to expect.

Here's another helpful hint. Turn off the TV and go to bed early before you start dozing off in the living room chair. You might be amazed at what happens when you least expect it.

Four More Wishes

Husband, here are four things that every woman wishes her husband knew.

Number One: *Always remember that sex for a woman is 90 percent mental.* What every woman wishes her husband would remember is that the most powerful sexual organ in her body is her mind. If a woman's mind is not prepared for sex, she cannot respond sexually. It doesn't matter what else you do with her body. She is not going to get there.

To be a great lover is to understand the most important part of our wife's sexual satisfaction is her mind. It is easy for a man, but it is not always as easy for a woman. God made us different. I apologize for using a cliché, but I don't know how to say this in a better way—men are like microwaves, and women are like Crock-Pots. They take time to warm up.

Men are not as complex. We have one switch that is either on or off. A woman has many mental and emotional switches that must be fine-tuned before she can hit the switch sexually. Her mind is more like an instrument panel. Men think in simple equations. "One plus one equals happy man," or "My wife and me is all I need."

Women, however, think in far more complex equations. God made them that way. The problem for a man is that the complex equations are always changing; they are never quite the same. When we think we have it all figured out, it changes the next time. This is part of the way God made a woman, and this is what keeps sex interesting and exciting over the course of marriage.

It's a constant process of learning and discovering the combination for the lock to your wife's garden. Be patient. Don't get frustrated when it takes time. Relax and have fun. You do not go straight for other parts of her body until her mind is fully ready and prepared.

Solomon started at the top, removing his bride's veil before he moved down. He did not start at the bottom and move up. He started by talking to her. A great sex life doesn't begin in the bedroom. It begins in the living room when you're just sitting on the couch together. It begins in the kitchen when you're doing the dishes together. It's about your ongoing interactions throughout the day, which brings me to the next point.

Number Two: *To satisfy your wife as her lover, it begins long before you get into the bedroom.* Every man likes to think of himself as a great lover, but the greatest lover who ever lived is Jesus. Jesus said He *"did not come to be served, but to serve, and give His life a ransom for many."* You cannot expect great sex at night if your wife says, "Honey, will you please remember to take out the trash?" Then you forget, and she ends up taking out the trash in the morning. You cannot expect your wife to act like a spring flower if you come home at night and blow in winter weather. The husband sets the atmosphere of the home. If you are distant all evening because your mind is on your job, the relationship feels cool, if not cold, to her. Then when it is time for bed, you get all warm and fuzzy. You can forget about it because you haven't prepared her along the way.

Being a great lover is displayed in how you talk to her and serve her. It is how you respond to her when she is not having one of her more lovable moments. You love her gently and unconditionally anyway. How you react and respond to her at breakfast might define what happens when you go to bed hours later.

Remember, a man's sexual energy is testosterone. This is why it is never a bad time for a man to have sex. Men are always ready, and somehow even after a long day, we find the energy. For a woman, it's about how you responded at breakfast. It was the text you sent her during the day and what happened when you greeted each other after work. The first twenty minutes when you come back together at the end of a long day is the most important part of your day, and it can define the rest of the evening.

Christa is a hard worker and keeps a clean house, but after our kids were grown, she went back to work outside the home. If I get home before her, I can set the atmosphere of my home by cleaning the kitchen. I don't want her to see a sink full of dishes as soon as she comes through the door.

This isn't about sex; it's about being a great lover. Jesus taught that to love someone is to serve them. It's learning how to be a great lover for your wife, and the overflow is in the bedroom. It is not about what you do in bed and your sexual prowess—it's knowing how to love her before you ever get to the bedroom.

Number Three: *Remember, women need to be aroused by foreplay.* I said earlier that men are like microwaves and women are like Crock-Pots. Women warm up far more slowly than men. A lot of men skip the "warmups" and then wonder why the main event doesn't feel like the main event.

In Song of Solomon, sex is repeatedly called "the garden." I love to garden. I know that if you want to pick the best fruit from the garden, it needs time, nurturing, fertilizer, water, and weeding—lots and lots of weeding. A garden takes work.

A frequent complaint of men is their wives do not respond sexually to them. It doesn't take much to discern that they have let the garden in their marriage become overgrown with weeds. Even though you haven't nurtured her, you expect to walk in and pick the best fruit of the garden. You are kidding yourself.

There are 14-foot-high weeds growing in your garden. You have neglected her emotionally, yet you expect her to respond sexually. It is impossible. You haven't watered the garden. You haven't fertilized the garden. Take care of your garden the way Solomon has taken care of his, and your wife will respond with the best fruit because that's the way God made her. Yes, foreplay begins long before you get in the bedroom, but the foreplay must continue in the bedroom.

I'm not going to draw a picture for you but do whatever she needs you to do to let her fully warm up. Communicate with her and don't try to read her mind. If you're not sure, ask her what's working and what she likes. When you get to know your wife, you'll figure out the combination of the lock on her garden, but don't be surprised if it changes without notice. That's okay. Take your time until you figure out what works for her.

Number Four: Affection is to her what sex is to her husband—one empowers the other. Sex alone is not what makes her feel loved and special. Sex is what comes after she feels loved. What makes her feel loved? A simple non-sexual touch that does not lead anywhere. The more affection she feels from her husband, the more she will naturally respond with sex. The more sexual intimacy he feels from his wife, the more he naturally responds with affection. It is the sex/affection cycle.

Five Ways to Improve

There are five ways married couples can immediately improve their sex life.

First, talk openly, honestly, and compassionately about your sexual needs, desires, and insecurities. Couples talk about everything under the sun, but many refuse to talk about their sex life. Years of disappointment and frustration can lead to division, silence, and resignation. What God meant for good can now be used by Satan for evil. Talk to each other compassionately. Give each other an abundance of grace. Talk about your insecurities and fantasies. If it's mutually pleasing, fully consensual, and not physically debilitating or unhealthy to either partner's body, I don't believe anything is off-limits before our God. Remember, we're not Puritans, we're Christians, and it is in the Bible. Go back and read Song of Solomon chapter 4 again if you don't believe me.

Second, start early and enjoy some spontaneity. Turn off late-night television and go to bed before you're exhausted. At a minimum, you are going to get a better night's sleep, and who knows what more could happen? Taking care of yourself physically will also have an impact on your sexual satisfaction.

Plan some special moments along the way for the two of you when you won't feel rushed, like a romantic weekend getaway or a staycation for a night or two at home when you've planned for someone else to take the kids. Then be ready to capitalize on the unplanned moments as well. Make time for spontaneity in the middle of a busy workweek. You don't always have time for a well-planned, four-course meal. Sometimes, you only have time for a Happy Meal at the drive-through.

Third, *get plenty of practice and have patience.* First Corinthians 7:1-5 teaches that having sex with your spouse is a responsibility we have in marriage as husbands and wives. God commands us to bless our spouse sexually and freely give them our bodies to enjoy. This biblical truth should not be used to coerce or manipulate your spouse for your own gratification. Yet Scripture is clear that we have a mutual responsibility in marriage. Your sexual relationship is like anything else—the more you practice, the better you get at it.

Movies will lie to you. They will have you think it is supposed to be explosive every time you get together. Your sex life is not a love scene from a movie with paid actors. Our sexualized culture has set many couples up for dissatisfaction and disappointment. One of the beautiful things about a couple in marriage is they get to practice until they get it right. It may take time for you to find the right combination, but eventually, two people who have been together and know each other intimately will find their rhythm if they don't give up.

I want to encourage young married couples that the best sex is not in your twenties or even your thirties. It's in your forties and fifties and, yes, even your sixties and beyond. My point is that the best sex happens after years of being with someone and knowing each other deeply. Movies glorify the one-night stand, the hookup, and sleeping with the mysterious stranger you only just met. Two strangers can have sex, but they cannot make love. They do not know each other. That's why, in the end, it always leaves people longing for more because that's how God made them.

Fourth, *get medical help if you need it.* Various forms of sexual dysfunction are common, especially as couples get older in years. But they are not uncommon even among younger couples. From P.E. to E.D. and various other common problems that can emerge in the bedroom, most of these symptoms can be clinically treated. Get over the embarrassment, and for the sake of your marriage, go see a doctor. Take the medicine. It's common for older couples to have less sex than they used to, but it will never stop being an important part of your relationship. Don't resign it.

Fifth, *pray together for God to give you a satisfying sex life.* You are not going to make God blush. Your Father in Heaven wants to give you a deeply fulfilling and satisfying sex life in marriage. Pray and ask God to bless this part of your marriage and thank Him for the gift He has given you.

I didn't consistently pray with my wife for many years in my marriage, even after I became a pastor. I didn't want to look stupid in front of her, which is why many men refuse to pray with their spouses. Praying is a deeply intimate act that we do together.

Eventually, I decided to pray with her every day. I will never forget what my wife said many years ago: "Phil, I want you to know that you are never more desirable to me than when you pray with me." (She said that with the "winky" eye.) I took that to heart, and we started praying even more.

9

WHEN YOU'VE LOST THAT LOVIN' FEELIN'

In Song of Solomon chapter 5, we find that all is not well in paradise. Time has passed, and Solomon and the Shulamite have been married for a while now. We don't know how long, but it's no longer their honeymoon night. They are somewhere beyond the seven-day wedding celebration, and they have settled into the rhythm of married life. It's probable that the stanza of the Song describing their honeymoon night in chapter 4 was added later after their wedding feast, and the stanza in chapter 5, was added later as well.

In chapter 5, Solomon describes in his typical poetic fashion what is probably their first married fight. It was enough of a defining moment in their marriage that he chose to record it for all generations. Conflict has entered their relationship. The honey seems to have leaked out after the honeymoon.

Conflict—An Inevitability

This is the most important issue for your marriage. Conflict is inevitable no matter how much you love each other. In times of conflict, we all want to win; but in marriage, you either both win or neither of you wins. It's never a win for anyone if it's not a win for everyone. It is crucial to learn how to have conflict in a healthy way that leads to a positive, happy outcome. What will define the success of your marriage the most is how you handle and navigate conflict because conflict is part of life.

> *I sleep, but my heart is awake; it is the voice of my beloved! He knocks, saying, "Open for me, my sister, my love, my dove, my perfect one; for my head is covered with dew, my locks with the drops of the night"* (Song of Solomon 5:2).

The Shulamite is awakened by Solomon who wants to come into her bed chamber, but the door is locked. He knocks saying, *"Open for me, my sister, my love, my dove, my beautiful one."* That is Hebrew for "Hey darling! I've got that lovin' feelin' and you know what that means!" She knows exactly what it means, and she responds in a not-so-romantic way that is Hebrew for "I have a headache." In verse 3, she says: *"I have taken off my robe; how can I put it on again? I have washed my feet; how can I defile them?"*

They lived in a time when married couples had separate sleeping chambers, especially a king and queen. When the king was feeling frisky, he would come to her sleeping chamber. Solomon knocked on her door. "Hello, darling. It is your hunka hunka burnin' love!" She flat-out turns him down. I personally suspect Solomon has come to her chamber to make up from a previous spat they had. Her response is to tell him to go away and let her sleep. She doesn't want to get out of bed and put her robe back on. Solomon is not that easily dissuaded. "Oh, come on, darling. I just want to talk. Honestly, I just want a little conversation." She responds, "Go away. I don't want to get out of bed and get my feet dirty. Let me get some sleep."

When the Shulamite rejects his invitation, it leads to conflict and separation. Again, this interaction could have been part of a previous conflict that appears to have been already in motion. Solomon is seeking reconciliation, but she is clearly not ready. Conflict can lead to separation in fellowship and relationships. We are about to see this couple's conflict resolution in verses 4 and 5. Conflict in marriage is inevitable, no matter how much you love each other.

My beloved put his hand by the latch of the door, and my heart yearned for him. I arose to open for my beloved, and my hands dripped with myrrh, my fingers with liquid myrrh, on the handles of the lock.

Solomon's response is amazing. Her door was made so Solomon could reach through and open it himself if he wanted to. He could have become angry and forced his way in, saying, "I am the king, and nobody says 'no' to me, not even you. I am here because it's my right, and you are my wife." He doesn't do any of that. He simply reaches through her door and rubs a little liquid myrrh on the inside of her doorknob.

Culturally, in Solomon's day, his response was like leaving a bouquet of flowers by her door. She understood exactly what he meant. As he left his calling card on her door, he was saying, "It is okay. I love you anyway." Instead of demanding his rights, he laid down his rights. Well done, Solomon! Played like a real man instead of a selfish adolescent child.

In marriage, how you respond in times of conflict will either lead to true restoration and conflict resolution or further tension and separation. Stop fighting for your rights and start fighting for your marriage. Seek to understand instead of seeking to be understood. In this case, the couple's conflict spilled over into their sex life, which is something a lot of couples struggle with. Sometimes the conflict has to do with sex itself and the expectations around sex that go unmet. This is why the apostle Paul writes:

> *Nevertheless, because of sexual immorality, let each man have his own wife, and let each woman have her own husband. Let the husband render to his wife the affection due her, and likewise also the wife to her husband. The wife does not have authority over her own body, but the husband does. And likewise the husband does not have authority over his own body, but the wife does. Do not deprive one another except with consent for a time, that you may give yourselves to fasting and prayer; and come together again so that Satan does not tempt you because of your lack of self-control* (1 Corinthians 7:2-5).

To be clear, Paul's reference to affection in this passage is not referring to a little peck on the cheek. He's referring to sexual affection. It is crucial to understand the expectations and our responsibilities to each other in marriage.

God's Word teaches us that in marriage, husbands have a responsibility to their wives, and wives have a responsibility to their husbands. Neither one has authority over their own body. This is what it means to be "one flesh," which is God's desire for our marriages (Matthew 19:6). We're not independent of each other. We're interdependent on each other because God's plan is for us to protect each other.

That is why Paul says to come together again so that Satan doesn't tempt you because of your lack of self-control. In other words, men have the responsibility of guarding their wives from sexual temptation in the same way wives have the responsibility of guarding their husbands from sexual temptation. We set up our spouse for temptation when we withhold affection—not just sexually but emotionally as well. Husband, you do that by the way you love and pour yourself into your wife. Wife, you are to help guard your husband from temptation by the way you love him and the way you freely give yourself to him.

> **We do not have a right to demand anything of the other.**
> **We only have the responsibility to give everything**
> **to each other.**

Solomon, in his infinite wisdom, did not demand anything from his wife. Instead, he freely laid down his rights for her. He laid down his need for her need. In marriage, when a man is laying down his life to meet the needs of his wife, and a woman is laying down her life to meet the needs of her husband, the result is a healthy, happy marriage until death do they part.

Every man, regardless of the era in which he lived, has always been the same. Rejection puts a big dent in our manhood. Solomon felt the sting of rejection. His wife's rejection would have come as a blow. It would have hurt him emotionally. He could respond by getting angry and demanding what he considered to be his right, or he could choose humility. His humble response to this rejection is what paved the path forward to reconciliation. Song of Solomon 5:6-8:

> *I opened for my beloved, but my beloved had turned away and was gone. My heart leaped up when he spoke. I sought him, but I could not find him; I called him, but he gave me no answer. The watchmen who went about the city found me. They struck me, they wounded me; the keepers of the walls took my veil away from me. I charge you, O daughters of Jerusalem, if you find my beloved, that you tell him I am lovesick!*

In verse 6, the Shulamite is describing another dream. Perhaps a dream she had this very night after Solomon left and she went back to sleep. This is a dream of love that is lost. We know it is a dream because no one would have struck the king's bride. Solomon was the most powerful man in the world at this time. The consequences would have been catastrophic for the perpetrator of such a reprehensible act.

This also speaks to how Jesus feels about you. He is the Bridegroom, and you are His bride. He loves and cares about you. If you want to get on the wrong side of Jesus, just come against His bride.

Appropriate Response

In verse 7, she is beating herself up in her dreams because she is feeling guilty about not getting up and opening the door. Solomon's humble response—leaving his calling card of myrrh—touched and broke her heart for her beloved. No matter how great a marriage you may have, there will always be times when your spouse lets you down and hurts you. We all have moments when we feel rejection, betrayal, hurt, or heartache. How you respond next will make the difference between how long you stay separated and how quickly your relationship is restored.

Solomon provided us with a textbook response as a Spirit-filled person who is led and controlled by the Spirit of God in times of conflict. Although not a New Testament believer, he reflects the fruit of the Spirit (Galatians 5:22-23).

First, he responded with gentle communication. He is filled with gentleness and self-control. Without saying a word, he spoke volumes. The most difficult thing to do when somebody has hurt you is not to strike back to hurt them too. When you react out of hurt and anger, you will always say things you regret. Words are something you can apologize for later, but they are impossible to take back. The best thing you can do is quietly retreat for a few minutes to pray.

Even better, during times of marital conflict, one of you needs to suggest that you both stop and pray before proceeding any further. Ask Jesus to take control of the situation. Ask Jesus to bind the enemy that has come to *"steal, kill, and destroy"* (John 10:10). Ask God to soften your hearts toward each other and grant you the gift of humility and repentance. Otherwise, the next thing you know, words are flying that you are going to regret and may not even mean. It is like lobbing verbal hand grenades into the middle of your marriage that will blow up everything—including each other. Your marriage is bleeding out, and you wonder why.

> Ask God to soften your hearts toward each other and grant you the gift of humility and repentance.

I was part of the Kansas City Police Department for years. I was often called to the scene of domestic violence or conflict. Everybody was yelling and screaming at each other. The younger officers would try to yell over them to quiet them down, and they would end up in a shouting match. I learned that instead of trying to yell louder than everyone else, it was more effective to speak calmly and quietly. "I hear you. Let's just talk," and this began to de-escalate the situation. This is important to remember during times of conflict. Just talk to each other.

When you're in a shouting match, you feel attacked and take a defensive posture. When that happens, the fight or flight response takes over. The other person is either going to fight or flee from the situation. Either way, you do not solve anything—but you do create a barrier that will only grow over time. This is why conflict can sometimes go on for years and years. And while you're attempting to pick up the broken pieces, it slowly ruins your fellowship and erodes your relationship.

Next, Solomon submitted to the needs of his wife over his own needs. Instead of making demands, he chose to leave quietly and not become angry or put her on a guilt trip. The essence of every marriage is about a man and a woman mutually submitting to one another.

The greatest chapter ever written in this marriage manual we call the Bible is Ephesians chapter 5. The apostle Paul begins his dissertation on marriage in verse 21: *"Submitting to one another in the fear of God."* Mutual submission is the key. When a husband and wife are both fully submitted to God, they are fully submitted to each other. The verse that follows is a favorite of Christian men:

> *Wives, submit to your own husbands, as to the Lord* (Ephesians 5:22).

While this verse is often quoted to illustrate the wife's biblical responsibility to submit to her husband, you can't fully apply verse 22 as intended unless we begin with verse 21. Husbands have the responsibility to submit as well. Submission, as God intended, is to be mutual between a husband and wife as they mutually submit to God the Father.

As your head naturally submits to the needs of your body, a husband, as the head, is to submit himself to the needs of his wife. As our bodies naturally submit to the lead of our heads, a wife should willingly submit herself to the lead of her husband. That is how God designed you to become one flesh in marriage, with the head and the body mutually submitted to one another. However, you cannot submit to each other if you are not truly submitted to God first.

It is an issue of your heart attitude toward God. The problem for many people is they aren't really submitted to Him. You don't know if you are submitted to God until He gives you something difficult to do that you don't want to do. That is the test. You know the most about your submission to God based on your submission to each other in marriage.

Resolution

So how do you resolve conflict when you're mutually submitted to each other? Remember, there is a portrait God wants your marriage to portray—one that illustrates your relationship with your heavenly Bridegroom. If the man is the head (Ephesians 5:23) and one flesh with his wife (Genesis 2:24), that means the woman is the body. Remember, the husband mirrors Christ, and the wife is a reflection of the Church—the bride and body of Christ.

Consider what God is teaching and ask yourself whether your body submits to your head, or your head submits to your body. You can't live without either of them. Your body submits to the direction of your head. If your head says, "Go this way," your feet follow. But your head never once thinks about its own needs. It is always thinking about the needs of the body. If your body is hungry, your head says, "Get some food." If your body is cold, your head says, "Get a blanket."

When both are submitting to each other, you have the kind of love that will last forever. If you don't have a submissive heart attitude toward God, you don't stand a chance of having it toward each other. Your home will be a war zone in constant chaos. This isn't about who has the stronger will and who has the harder head. This is about a heart attitude that says, "I want what you want more than I want what I want." I'm convinced if we would just live out these two verses in marriage it would revolutionize every aspect of our lives and marriage.

Let nothing be done through selfish ambition or conceit, but in lowliness of mind let each esteem others better than himself. Let each of you look out not only for his own interests, but also for the interests of others (Philippians 2:3-4).

This is what Solomon did. Instead of being prideful and arrogant about his needs and rights, he chose humility and her needs and rights. She needed sleep. When you learn how to communicate gently and rationally, coupled with a heart attitude of submission, your marriage will have a harmonious rhythm until death do you part.

Last, he responded with affection in the face of rejection. This would have been even more difficult for Solomon. He was the king, and nobody ever told him, "No." Whatever he saw was his. Whatever he wanted, he could have. There were no negotiations. He was a monarch—sovereign over a large and powerful kingdom. His was not a government of democratic processes. He could have ruled over his marriage in the same manner, but during this time in his life, he was far too humble and wise to do that. This king was not a typical king. Throughout the Song of Solomon, he was a picture of Jesus, who was both a Shepherd and our King.

As our Shepherd, He laid down his life to meet our needs. As our King, He has the authority to exercise righteous rulership over our lives. This night, in Song of Solomon chapter 5, he came not as the king, but as the shepherd to lay down his life humbly to meet the needs of his bride. That brings us back to Ephesians 5:33, where the apostle Paul sums up his great dissertation on marriage:

Nevertheless let each one of you in particular so love his own wife as himself, and let the wife see that she respects her husband.

With that verse, Paul tells us what is in the heart of most men and women. She longs to be loved, cherished, and treasured. He longs to be respected, esteemed, and admired. I shared this in an earlier chapter, but I cannot overemphasize this vital truth. This is the rhythm of love that lasts a lifetime. When he gives affection, it naturally leads to desire on the part of his wife to give him admiration. Admiration is more than something you feel; it is something you do. When you put it in motion, the emotion will follow. This is the cycle Solomon put in motion when he died to his own needs to meet the needs of his bride.

The final verses in chapter 5 say it all. Her girlfriends ask her, *"Oh, fairest among women? What is your beloved more than another beloved, that you so charge us?"* They are asking Solomon's bride what makes her husband so special. Her response is the most profound description of her admiration anywhere in Song of Solomon.

> *My beloved is white and ruddy, chief among ten thousand. His head is like the finest gold; his locks are wavy, and black as a raven. His eyes are like doves by the rivers of waters, washed with milk, and fitly set. His cheeks are like a bed of spices, banks of scented herbs. His lips are lilies, dripping liquid myrrh. His hands are rods of gold set with beryl. His body is carved ivory inlaid with sapphires. His legs are pillars of marble set on bases of fine gold. His countenance is like Lebanon, excellent as the cedars. His mouth is most sweet, yes, he is altogether lovely. This is my beloved, and this is my friend, O daughters of Jerusalem!*

She is saying he is the hottest hunk of Hebrew masculinity she has ever laid eyes on. She just wants to grab him, kiss him, and wrap her arms around him. She describes him as humble, noble, honorable, handsome, and strong. And most of the words that come out of his mouth are sweet and beautiful, *"like lilies, dripping with liquid myrrh."*

Solomon's gentle communication and sacrificial love set his bride's response in motion. He loved her even when she was not that lovable, and it made her more lovable. The result was she began to have loving feelings for her husband again.

Whether it is conflict in marriage or conflict in other relationships, the principles are the same. In my marriage, I have learned over the years that what you fight about is usually not the real issue. It is merely a symptom of a deeper issue. My wife is an angel, but when she gets grouchy with me, it is usually my fault. I have not done a good job of making her feel loved and cherished. That is the real issue.

Overwhelmingly, the number one complaint of men who come to me because they are unhappy in their marriage is their wives don't respect them. Whatever the other issues may be, the real issue is that he wants the admiration and esteem of his wife. There are certainly times he doesn't deserve it because there are times when he doesn't act respectably.

In the same way, a husband is to love his wife unconditionally. When a wife respects her husband unconditionally, he will reflect more of those attributes. When all is said and done, during times of conflict, getting it right is far more important than figuring out who is right.

There are things my wife and I will never fully agree on. Real unity and restoration do not demand that you fully agree on everything. What matters most is seeking to understand. It doesn't usually matter who is right and who is wrong. Do you want to be right, or do you want to be restored?

—10—

HOW TO GET BACK THAT
LOVIN' FEELIN'

In Song of Solomon chapter 5, our lovebirds had their first fight, and paradise was lost. The good news is in chapter 6, we see paradise regained. Falling in love is easy; staying in love is a choice. But what do you do when you've lost your love for each other?

No doubt you've heard the phrase, "Love is a feeling," as well as the response that it's more than a feeling. Both statements are true because love is something you feel *and* something you do. Love is an emotion, but it's so much more than an emotion—it's a motion. This is the highest form of love that Scripture talks about repeatedly. It's God's love.

The Greeks had several words for love at the time the New Testament was penned by Christ's apostles. One of the Greek words for love is *eros* from which we get the word "erotic." This speaks of the romantic, sexual love felt between a man and a woman. When the New Testament talks about love, it's almost always *agape* love, which speaks of Christ's love for us. It's a sacrificial kind of love. It's not a feeling but a choice. Only when agape love is at work in your marriage, will eros be working too.

When you've lost that lovin' feeling, choose to put your love in motion to get back the emotion. You need to go back and do the things that made you fall in love. If you wait to feel the emotion, you may never put your love into action. By choosing agape love, eros love will eventually follow. Eros is a feeling, while agape is a choice. This is an important distinction.

Eros is a feeling—agape is a choice.

You do not always choose to fall in love, but there comes a time in every marriage when you must choose to stay in love. No married couple has ever spent 50 years of uninterrupted marital bliss. There have been some rocky moments and difficult days along the way. The real miracle is not falling in love but staying in love after two people have been staring at each other for 50 years. What is their secret? They chose to stay when it would have been easier to walk away. God blesses that choice by following it with emotion.

Put your love into action, and you'll get back that lovin' feeling.

Song of Solomon chapter 6 begins with the Shulamite's girlfriends asking, *"Where has your beloved gone, O fairest among women? Where has your beloved turned aside, that we may seek him with you?"* She responds in verses 2-3:

> *My beloved has gone to his garden, to the beds of spices, to feed his flock in the gardens, and to gather lilies. I am my beloved's, and my beloved is mine. He feeds his flock among the lilies.*

In the verses that follow, Solomon cannot say enough about the love of his life.

> *O my love, you are as beautiful as Tirzah, lovely as Jerusalem, awesome as an army with banners!*

Tirzah is an oasis in the Judean desert, just outside of Jerusalem. Solomon tells her that she is his oasis. In the middle of the scorching desert, she is like a cool drink of water: *"Lovely as Jerusalem, awesome as an army with banners!"* He describes his wife as a warrior princess who fights with him in battle.

Life is warfare. Yet, like the stronghold of Jerusalem with its walled fortifications, his wife provides him with a safe place to retreat. In verses 5 and 6, he says:

> *Turn your eyes away from me, for they have overcome me. Your hair is like a flock of goats going down from Gilead. Your teeth are like a flock of sheep which have come up from the washing; every one bears twins, and none is barren among them.*

He is so mesmerized by this woman, that just one look into her eyes makes his heart melt. She has undone her hair, and it is falling on her shoulders. If the next verse sounds familiar, it's because these are the same words he said to her on their honeymoon night—which tells us that the "honey" is back, and it is a second honeymoon. They have that lovin' feeling again because they put their love into action.

In chapter 5, he responded to her rejection with affection, which elicited her admiration and set the stage for the restoration of their relationship.

Solomon continues in verses 7 through 9:

> *Like a piece of pomegranate are your temples behind your veil. There are sixty queens and eighty concubines, and virgins without number. My dove, my perfect one, is the only one, the only one of her mother, the favorite of the one who bore her. The daughters saw her and called her blessed, the queens and the concubines, and they praised her.*

Even her temples are sensual and a place of seduction for him. Solomon tells her there may be a lot of other queens and virgins and concubines, but she is the only one he sees. She is far above them all. He does not stop there. He continues in verse 10, saying his beloved is as *"fair as the moon, clear as the sun."* Basically, he's saying her love shines bright, and she lights up his life. After their spat, the Shulamite wants to know if their love is still alive. She is going down to the garden to see if the vineyard is in bloom which is, of course, a euphemism for their sex life.

> *I went down to the garden of nuts to see the verdure of the valley, to see whether the vine had budded and the pomegranates had bloomed. Before I was even aware, my soul had made me as the chariots of my noble people.*

In verse 12, Solomon gives her a place of honor and puts her on a pedestal. No one rode in the king's chariot without having such an honored position.

Husbands, take note. We are a picture of Solomon and Christ—the Shepherd and the King. As such, we are also to treat our wives like queens by putting them on a pedestal and giving them the highest place of honor.

> *Husbands, likewise, dwell with them* [your wives] *with understanding, giving honor to the wife...* (1 Peter 3:7).

She is now riding in his chariot, and Solomon and his friends say in verse 13, *"Return, return, O Shulamite; return, return that we may look upon you!"* They are cheering and praising her for her beauty, honor, and virtue.

We have come to the end of chapter 6, and there are only two chapters left. They have now gone through all the phases of their relationship. From friendship and infatuation to falling in love and getting married to the storming and norming of marriage, we have seen it all. Their love has clearly matured. It's far beyond mere infatuation with its fickle emotions. It has matured now into true love that will last a lifetime.

We don't know how long they have been married by the time we get to chapter 6, but it is probably decades. While I have called her the Shulamite from the very beginning of this book, this is the first time she is ever called such in Song of Solomon. Scholars do not agree on the location of Shulem from which she gets this title. Some argue for a location as far away as Lebanon, an ancient kingdom on the Mediterranean immediately north of Israel, whose modern nation still bears its name. Others argue for the town of Shunem, which was in the land grant of Issachar north of Mount Gilboa in the Jezreel Valley.

While the exact location has been lost, we know that *Shulamite* is a title that means "peaceful." This woman has brought great peace to Solomon, and they are now at peace with each other.

> The goal of every marriage is to become one flesh, not just physically—that is easy—but to truly become one body emotionally, spiritually, and mentally.

They have reached a place in their relationship where they are practically what they were already positionally. The moment you get married and say, "I do," God no longer sees two of you. He only sees one. The goal of every marriage is to become one flesh, not just physically—that is easy—but to truly become one body emotionally, spiritually, and mentally. While it happens instantly in God's eyes, positionally it takes a lifetime to grow into true oneness as He intended. This couple is now enjoying the fruit of committed love.

It is not a coincidence that *Shulamite* is the feminine form of the masculine name, *Solomon.* Similar to Phillip and Phyllis, Daniel and Danielle, or Robert and Roberta. Shulem was a place, but it is also a person. This woman's title is the "Shulamite," which no doubt comes from the place of her birth. But more importantly, they share the same name because they share the same heavenly Father. Finally, they are one person—truly living as one body in complete unity.

Chapter 6 concludes with the Shulamite saying, "*What would you see in the Shulamite—as it were, the dance of the two camps?*" They are seen now as two camps dancing together. After years of marriage, they have mastered the rhythm of marriage—how to move together rather than stumbling all over each other.

They know each other's moves and what they are going to do even before they do it. They are now moving together as one couple, one family, one body in unity. That is the goal when there has been separation. Their marriage has been restored, and they are enjoying the fruit of their garden of marriage. They have learned how to work through their conflicts. God did not make us cookie-cutter people. We all have our strengths and weaknesses, callings and giftings. God gave them to us to complement each other.

Points to Ponder

The following are some things to think about that will help you and your spouse go the distance like our lovebirds.

In times of hurt and frustration, do not stay angry; instead, respond spiritually. Anger is the emotional response to being wounded or hurt. In far too many marriages, when anger is not dealt with properly, it becomes bitterness. You may actually be angry with your spouse right now. Some have been married and angry for years, and now you're just going through the motions.

Anger, if not dealt with, will turn into bitterness, and bitterness can become ugly and hurtful. Forgiveness is always more for you than it is for them. When you begin to set them free, you become free as well. This is why Jesus says, *"Pray for your enemies."* In the heat of the moment, turn to God and give your anger to Him. When you do, you will come under the control of the Holy Spirit.

> *But the fruit of the Spirit is love, joy, peace, longsuffering, kindness, goodness, faithfulness, gentleness, self-control. Against such there is no law* (Galatians 5:22-23).

The moment you give your anger to God, the fruit of the Holy Spirit begins to flow into your life. Do you need patience with someone in your life? God has what you need. Do you need love in your life? Do you need to get back that lovin' feeling? It is not a coincidence that "love" tops the list of the life-transforming fruit of the Holy Spirit. The Greek word translated as *love* here is agape, not eros.

Remember, lead with agape, and you will get back eros. When you respond in a way that is godly and Christlike, everything begins to change. You are positioning yourself to work through the conflict so no one loses and everybody wins.

> *Be angry, and do not sin: do not let the sun go down on your wrath, nor give place to the devil* (Ephesians 4:26-27).

The apostle Paul teaches that when you and your spouse go to bed angry at each other, you literally invite the devil to snuggle in between you all night long. You marinate in that all night. When you wake up, you are now ten times more ticked off. Deal with it before you go to bed. It does not mean you must completely resolve the conflict, but you can deal with the anger.

God, take this anger from me and help me
to deal with this properly.

Next, continually give an abundance of grace and forgiveness. King Solomon is our blueprint for restoration. Solomon
and the Shulamite came back together after rejection and separation because Solomon responded with affection even when
he did not feel it. His spouse naturally admired his humility, and
that brought them back together for restoration. Somewhere
along the way, there had to be grace and forgiveness. He had
to forgive his wife for the rejection and the wound inflicted on
his heart.

In a healthy marriage, grace and forgiveness are received
and given almost daily. I used to think that in a healthy marriage, you would never have to say, "I'm sorry" because you
would never hurt each other or get angry with each other. I
thought you would never need to apologize because you just
knew what to do. How naïve I was.

The reality is that even in a truly healthy marriage, you will
get angry. You will get hurt. You will need to quickly ask for
grace and forgiveness and be quick to give it. There will be conflict, but it doesn't have to lead to separation, devastation, and
heartache. God wants to bring restoration. That means you are
going to give and receive forgiveness on a regular basis—perhaps even daily or weekly because we're going to hurt each
other, sometimes even unwittingly.

And be kind to one another, tenderhearted, forgiving one
another, even as God in Christ forgave you (Ephesians
4:32).

The apostle Paul is saying we need to start with the basics—
Relationships 101. We are often nicer to people we barely

know than the person we married. God has forgiven you, and He expects you to do the same. When you keep a short list of grievances and quickly seek and give forgiveness, you can come back together quickly instead of being separated.

I used to have this conversation repeatedly with my wife. She would say something like, "Phil, do you realize what you just did? Do you understand what just happened?" Most of the time my answer was, "No." She would respond with, "Well, this is what just happened, and honestly, it made me feel this way, and it was a little bit insensitive. And you may not have realized it." At one time, the younger Phil would immediately defend himself. "Wait a minute. I didn't mean to do anything to you. What are you talking about? You shouldn't feel that way."

An older and wiser Phil has learned to take responsibility quickly. "I am so sorry. I didn't know." This is how you start to do the dance that Solomon and his bride learned. It takes time—maybe even years—but eventually, you learn what to do and what not to do. When that happens, you find yourself moving in unity with your spouse instead of unwittingly walking all over each other. "Honey, do you know how that made me feel?" And in response, "I'm so sorry. I acted like an insensitive jerk. Will you please forgive me?"

Also, learn to communicate calmly. Once you start yelling and screaming, neither of you is listening. It's over. Seek to understand before being understood. Take a breath, step back, and try to understand instead of forming your next thought while your spouse is talking. If you're already thinking about what you are going to say next, you're not listening. You are looking for the zinger that is going to prove you're right.

If you're the kind of person who always has to be right, you will never have a healthy friendship, relationship, or marriage. In the end, it cannot be about proving who is right. It must be about saying, "Honey, let's get this right." You might learn something in the process.

Seek to understand before seeking to be understood and communicate gently.

Under the inspiration of the Holy Spirit, King Solomon wrote in Proverbs 27:15, "*A continual dripping on a very rainy day and a contentious woman are alike.*" The average woman loves her husband and doesn't mean to be contentious, but a contentious response will make most men feel like they are five years old and being scolded by their mother. They will simply tune their wife out. Never underestimate the sensitivity of the male ego. God gave it to him, and not all ego is sinful, but it can quickly morph into sin. A man will naturally do whatever it takes to hang on to a little swag, even if it means retreating from his wife.

As a married man, the apostle Peter understood how a wife can influence her husband to become more admirable even when he's not acting admirably. He wrote in 1 Peter 3:1:

> *Wives, likewise, be submissive to your own husbands, that even if some do not obey the word, they, without a word, may be won by the conduct of their wives.*

He had some choice words for husbands as well in 1 Peter 3:7:

> *Husbands, likewise, dwell with them with understanding, giving honor to the wife, as to the weaker vessel, and as being heirs together of the grace of life, that your prayers may not be hindered.*

Peter's advice to women is that if you will *live* the Word, your husband can be transformed *by* the Word, without saying a word. You transform your husband by letting God transform you. Words don't usually work on men, but a humble heart will make an indelible impact.

This doesn't mean you allow yourself to become a doormat, and it especially doesn't mean you allow him to bully or abuse you. Peter is not talking about such extreme situations. He is talking about a man who loves his wife but is not living a *godly* life. He might not even be a believer. If he is a Christian, he's not stepping up to his God-given role as a servant-leader in his home. Peter is reminding women that men are influenced more by what they see than anything their wives can say.

Then Peter turns to men and tells them to treat their wives in the same manner—walking in humility, understanding her needs, and putting her first.

Only God can change your spouse, so let God change you.

Speak and seek a resolution prayerfully. The problem is that too often men don't like to pray with their spouse. It makes us feel vulnerable and uncomfortable. It was years into our marriage before I would pray with my wife. I would pray by myself in private, but I didn't pray with her. I was a SWAT cop and had the courage to kick down a door not knowing what was on the other side, but I was afraid to pray with my wife.

There is something about being vulnerable with your wife that can make a man feel insecure. If you will get on your knees and make time to pray together, you will be amazed at how much your relationship will deepen. God will start to move your hearts in unity, and your conflict will not be what it used to be.

*It really comes down to giving and receiving
an abundance of grace.*

As you go through life together, there are times when you need to give more grace than others. Women often talk about mood swings because of PMS. My wife knows the later it gets on a Saturday, the more grace I need. I have PMS: Pre-Message Syndrome. Mentally, I'm no longer present as I begin to focus on Sunday.

There have been times when my wife has been talking to me on a Saturday afternoon and stopped mid-sentence and said, "You're not listening to me, are you?" It used to irritate her, but now she just says, "You're preaching, aren't you?" She now knows I'm not trying to ignore her, and she extends a lot of space and grace. I'm sure all the husbands and wives reading this have their own version and know what I mean.

Sometimes you are both just exhausted at the end of a long day, and you're empty physically and emotionally. You're tapped out. That is when you can start to get under each other's skin. Give each other grace at times like this. Don't let it spill over into the next day. Sometimes when you're not at your best, the best thing you can do for your marriage is just go to bed.

Overcoming Strongholds

Sometimes, serious conflict may arise in marriage—not the kind that a good night's sleep can help resolve. I'm talking about conflict sown through repeated patterns of sin, which can cause a deep chasm of relational and emotional pain.

For example, an affair is like a hatchet that can deeply wound a marriage with a single blow. Sometimes, it's not a single blow from a hatchet, but rather it's death by a thousand cuts. Your marriage is slowly bleeding out over the course of weeks, months, and even years. I'm talking about small and sometimes subtle patterns of sin and dysfunction that don't appear to be a real threat at first but have a dangerous effect over time.

Repeated sin, no matter how subtle, always gives Satan a toehold. That toehold eventually becomes a handhold, and that handhold eventually becomes a stronghold.

Satan Had a Stronghold in My Marriage

I know what I'm talking about because there was once a satanic stronghold on my own marriage. You've heard me say that disobedience to God while dating will bring dysfunction into your marriage. I certainly brought it into mine. It has been years now, but I still reflect every March when our marriage was forever changed. It was because something changed in me. Christa and I have been married more than 30 years now, but this pivotal moment came in March, in year 14 of our marriage. By this time, I had resigned from my career in law enforcement and had answered the call of God upon my life to pastor God's people and preach His Word. I'm now convinced Satan was attempting to destroy my ministry by slowly destroying our marriage.

Everyone at the time would have seen us as a happy, healthy couple. For the most part, this would have been true, but as the years went by, we were becoming more and more unhappy and unhealthy. I remember being in this season of life and driving to the marriage retreat our church was hosting that year. We had a guest speaker coming, dozens of couples had signed up, and I was praying God would do a wonderful work in all of their marriages.

I commented to Christa on the way there, "We already have a pretty good marriage." What I was really saying was "Mirror,

mirror on the wall, am I doing any good at all?" My *mirror* just sat there staring straight ahead. I repeated what I'd said, only this time I made a question out of it: "We have a pretty good marriage, don't we?" Silence. I was hurt and irritated by the time we got to the retreat. The simple truth is Christa had said a lot by not saying anything at all, and I knew it was true.

You see, I hadn't connected all the dots, and I was choosing to live in denial. Like most men, I had convinced myself that things were better than they were and that whatever problems we had were as much my wife's issues as they were mine. Unfortunately, I almost broke my *mirror* before God would finally break me. Today, I'm so thankful He did.

The sinful pattern that emerged by the fourteenth year of our marriage began very subtly. It might have only materialized once or twice a year in the early years. As the years went by, it began happening more frequently. Eventually, it was monthly, and by the fourteenth year, it was every week—usually right before the weekend when we should have been enjoying some extra time together.

The pattern went something like this: Christa would say or do something that hurt me. It usually was not her fault. It could have been something she had done unwittingly, but it was something she said or did that made me feel weak, disrespected, or unwanted. I'm sharing this with you now because this pattern plagued our marriage, and it's the same behavior that troubles many marriages.

Remember, a man will retreat from anything that makes him feel weak. God made men with a need to be strong and feel strong. He wants to feel like a man. He has two mirrors—his work and his wife. I felt weak and inadequate in my marriage, like I was never enough. Again, it was not her fault. It was something broken in me that only Jesus could heal.

A man will do one of two things when he feels weak around a woman relationally. He will either blow up and get mad to regain control, or he will retreat emotionally. Occasionally I would blow up and get angry. But most of the time, I would just retreat emotionally and give my wife the silent treatment. The more I was hurt, the longer I wouldn't talk to her—sometimes for several days at a time.

At the time, I was never consciously aware that in my sinful, broken self, it was my way of punishing her. I loved her. All I knew was that I was hurting, and it was my way of trying to recover my strength when she made me feel weak. I was trying to convince myself I didn't need her by withdrawing from her. I was trying to regain control and recover my broken masculinity.

The reality was that I was taking life from my marriage by taking life from my wife. Satan had absolutely cracked the code of our marriage to bring about our slow destruction. If God hadn't done what He did in our lives in March 2006, who knows where we would be today. Had the pattern continued, we would either be divorced or so broken we would be two married zombies just going through the motions.

A Slow but Steady Death

I didn't have the maturity then to understand what I know now. All along, I wanted my wife to want me the way I wanted her. I wanted to be desired the way I desired her. I wanted her to pursue me the way I pursued her. I knew my wife loved me, but I never felt like she was in love with me.

As human beings, we react to pain without thinking about it. If you accidentally place your hand on a hot stove, you instinctively remove it. We react to all pain in the same way, whether it's physical or emotional pain. I didn't know at the time that I was reacting to pain that had been buried deep inside of me since before I met Christa. I know now that I was reacting out of my own insecurity and broken masculinity. Christa had my heart, but I wasn't sure I had hers. And it was becoming a self-fulfilling prophecy.

One night, lying in bed after the lights were out, I don't even remember now what was said, but whatever it was, it hit my trigger. I reacted in the same way I had countless times before. I rolled over on my side, turning my back to her. I was hurt. I was angry, and I was going to give her the silent treatment. I was going to sleep angry, and I was going to wake up angry. I was not going to talk to her, maybe for several days. Then I heard my wife quietly sobbing in the darkness, and it broke my heart.

Year after year, month after month, season after season, I would retreat. I knew I was hurting, but I had no idea how badly I was hurting her. I was trying to save my life because, during those moments, I felt like I was dying inside. In trying to save myself in those moments of pain, I had no idea that I was taking the life of my bride. My marriage was slowly dying. That night, I realized for the first time how much I was hurting her.

We are never less desirable to our wives than when we quit talking and stop listening to them. It never worked because Christa didn't know what to do. So, in the end, she would wait me out. Eventually, I would get over it and talk to her again, but each time I drained a little more life from our marriage.

As I lay in bed listening to my wife sobbing, I distinctly heard the Holy Spirit say to me, "If you do not take care of her, you could lose her." My heart was broken. Instead of turning *away*, for the first time I chose to turn *in*. It is crucial for you to hear this! For the first time, I turned toward the pain instead of turning away. I said, "Honey, I am so sorry for what I have done to you. If you will forgive me, I promise to love you for the rest of my life."

Up to that point, I was trying to save myself. I was trying to avoid the pain. But that night, for the first time, I chose the nails. That is the night I learned what it means in Ephesians 5:25, *"Husbands, love your wives, just as Christ also loved the church and gave Himself for her."* I would have told you that I was a great Ephesians 5:25 kind of husband and would give my life for my wife.

The question is not whether you will die for your bride but whether you will live for her. I realized up to that point, I had tried to save my life instead of truly giving my life. I was trying to avoid the nails and protect myself from pain.

> *I got the wife I always wanted when I became the man God always wanted.*

That night I chose to die so that I could live for my bride, and everything changed! I got a new marriage without getting a new mate because God got a new man. Years later, it has never been the same. What today amounts to a few seconds, or at most a few minutes of silence between us, at one time would have been days. We still have conflict; we still have difficult moments. It is a part of all relationships. But instead of turning away, we now turn in and talk about the conflict, communicate gently, and listen carefully rather than becoming angry and responding in our fallen, sinful flesh.

It wasn't until weeks after God brought revival to our marriage in March of 2006 that I connected the dots. After much prayerful introspection with the *Wonderful Counselor* of Isaiah 9:6, God reminded me of some painful memories that I hadn't thought about for years.

Pain on the Inside Becomes Patterns on the Outside

Truthfully, I'd forgotten these painful memories in my mind, but they had deeply shaped my heart. Why did I react like this repeatedly over the course of so many years? Why did I have a trigger that only Christa could flip so easily? What was my source of insecurity when Christa had only ever proven her fidelity, love, and loyalty as my bride?

I told you earlier that disobedience when you're dating will lead to dysfunction when you're married. In the opening pages of this book, I told you I started dating way too early—long before I had the maturity to be in a romantic relationship. I had my first girlfriend before I even had hair on my legs and my second shortly after. I still had a child's heart while playing a grown-up game. That child's heart was broken, not only once, but twice. While still in adolescence, two girls had broken my heart, and my child's heart broke hard—it shattered into a thousand pieces.

I often hear parents say, "Well these teenage romances are just part of growing up." I will argue that they don't have to be if we teach our children how to guard their hearts before marriage so they can fully give their hearts away after marriage. What I know now is those moments of rejection and "lost love" in my adolescence were deeply traumatic.

My injured heart responded by making idols. As a young person, the idols of my heart became females, football, and fun. I became really good at getting all I wanted from all three, but of course, it was still never enough. Only Jesus could heal my heart, and only the truth could set me free.

The lies we believe the earliest are the lies that run the deepest and last the longest. The lies I began believing in adolescence, after feeling the pain of rejection, are the lies I believed into adulthood. They had unconsciously shaped my relation-ship with my wife for years. "You're not good enough. You will never measure up. You will never make a girl happy. You aren't handsome enough. You aren't man enough." I had no idea that when I married my wife, I still had the broken heart of a middle school child.

What I know now is all the years of giving Christa the silent treatment were driven by my own insecurity. I had married the girl voted best looking by our senior class. She was the one all the guys wanted to date. You would think that would have been enough to affirm my broken sense of masculinity, but when I pursued her my senior year, she "friend-zoned" me after only three dates.

Deep down, I think I wondered if marrying her was a fluke—like maybe someday she would realize she had made a mistake, and I wasn't enough. The lies we believe become a counterfeit reality. They were becoming a self-fulfilling prophecy. Satan has a way of crafting the bait we're most apt to take, but Jesus said, *"The truth shall set you free,"* and He brought healing to my broken, sinful heart.

The key to healing is to embrace the way of Calvary and the Cross—not merely the one on which Christ died—but the one on which you die. Only by way of the crucifixion do you get to the joy of the resurrection.

That's what I did in March 2006. God brought a resurrec-tion, and with it came a lasting transformation. As you choose the nails, you give life to your spouse and your marriage. If you want your marriage to live again, there can be a resurrection, but only after a crucifixion. Two people must go to a burial, and it must be yours.

If you go to your own funeral and choose to take the nails and embrace the crucifixion, God has the power to bring about resurrection, restoration, redemption, and reconciliation. He can take what was lost and restore it. He can breathe new life into your dead, loveless marriage.

Today is the day when everything can change in your marriage. It changed for me when I became the man God wanted. In return, I got the wife I always wanted.

You can get a new marriage without getting a new mate.

11

THE GARDENER

By the time we get to Song of Solomon chapter 7, the fruit of marriage is in full bloom. We don't know how much time has passed, but it is evident that this couple has now been married for a very long time. Solomon obviously added to this Song as the years went by. Their love has grown to full maturity.

After you plant a tree, you nurture it, and eventually you can harvest its fruit. Your best days as a married couple are not on your honeymoon—you are just getting started. Your best days are not in year one or year two when you are still that little tree. The real fruit of marriage happens when you could have walked away, but you chose to stay. It takes years for love to reach full maturity and for you to come to appreciate each other's deepest beauty.

How beautiful are your feet in sandals, O prince's daughter! The curves of your thighs are like jewels, the work of the hands of a skillful workman. Your navel is a rounded goblet; it lacks no blended beverage. Your waist is a heap of wheat set about with lilies. Your two breasts are like two fawns, twins of a gazelle. Your neck is like an ivory tower, your eyes like the pools in Heshbon by the gate of Bath Rabbim. Your nose is like the tower of Lebanon which looks toward Damascus. Your head crowns you like Mount Carmel, and the hair of your head is like purple; a king is held captive by your tresses. How fair and how pleasant you are, O love, with your delights! This stature of yours is like a palm tree, and your breasts like its clusters. I said, "I will go up to the palm tree, I will take hold of its branches." Let now your breasts be like clusters of the vine, the fragrance of your breath like apples, and the roof of your mouth like the best wine (Song of Solomon 7:1-9).

Solomon once again describes his bride—with a notable change. Every other time, he describes his wife's beauty from the head down. Now after decades of marriage, he begins with her feet and works up. He is seeing beauty where he never saw it before.

The first thing he says is, *"How beautiful are your feet in sandals."* Personally, I think feet are the ugliest part of the human anatomy but not Solomon. This man is still so mesmerized by the beauty of his bride that he sees it even in her feet. And he is just getting started. He was initially attracted to her because of her outward beauty. Now, after all these years, he is drawn to her inward beauty.

"Your navel is like a round goblet. It lacks no blended beverage." Ancient Hebrews considered the navel or the belly as part of a person's inward being. They used the term "bowels" or belly of a person like we would refer to their heart. Solomon is saying he sees her heart, and it is beautiful. He says her waist is *"like a heap of wheat."* In Solomon's day, wheat and wine were commodities of the wealthy. Solomon now sees her innermost being as full of wealth and beauty. He is complimenting not merely what she looks like outwardly but who she is inwardly. Because their love has reached maturity, he can now fully appreciate the depth of his wife's beauty.

In verse 3, Solomon once again compares her breasts to two fawns and twins of a gazelle. Solomon is practicing something he personally writes in Proverbs 5:18-19: *"Let your fountain be blessed, and rejoice in the wife of your youth. As a loving deer and a graceful doe, let her breasts satisfy you at all times; and always be enraptured with her love."*

In verse 4, he is complimenting this woman's inner strength. With a neck like an *"ivory tower,"* she is a woman with a backbone. Next, he compares her eyes to the pools of Heshbon that were known for their pristine water. The eyes are the window to the soul. He is saying to her, "I see purity and a woman at peace. When I look into your eyes, I see virtue and honor."

He continues comparing her nose to the tower of Lebanon—a watch tower in Jerusalem. From that high tower, they could stand guard and post a watch for their enemies. It looked toward Lebanon to the north of Israel because historically, Israel's enemies came down from the north. In essence, Solomon is saying, "I trust you implicitly. I know you always have my back. You are always facing behind me because you care about me and love me. You do not want anything to harm me." He next moves to her head and compares it to Mount Carmel. He is captivated by her tresses that are "like purple"— the color of royalty.

In verse 7, he likens her to a palm tree and her breasts to its clusters. In their day, palm trees were valuable for their coconuts, but they needed a male and female to bear fruit. Someone would climb to the top of the male tree and take hold of the flower containing the pollen. Then they would climb to the top of the female tree where they would deposit the pollen in its flowers so it would bear fruit. Solomon is saying something along the lines of, "I want to pollinate you." Husband, take note—never stop flirting with your wife.

Then he says, *"Let now your breasts be like clusters of the vine, the fragrance of your breath like apples and the roof of your mouth like the best wine."* Clearly, this couple is now making out.

It takes years for your love to grow to the deepest bond of intimacy. Solomon concludes his assessment by saying just like the best wine takes time, the absolute best time is when you give your love long enough to bear the very best fruit. He likens it to the fruit of the vine. Just like that fruit takes time to mature, a couple's love also takes time to fully mature and bloom.

What God promised them in the early days of their relationship, they are now living out beautifully in the latter years of their marriage. Repeatedly in Song of Solomon, he sees his relationship and marriage as a garden and his wife as a vineyard. Gardens and vineyards take time to mature. They need constant nurturing and work before they yield their very best fruit.

The Shulamite responds in verses 9-13:

> *The wine goes down smoothly for my beloved, moving gently the lips of sleepers. I am my beloved's, and his desire is toward me. Come, my beloved, let us go forth to the field; let us lodge in the villages. Let us get up early to the vineyards; let us see if the vine has budded, whether the grape blossoms are open, and the pomegranates are in bloom. There I will give you my love. The mandrakes give off a fragrance, and at our gates are pleasant fruits, all manner, new and old, which I have laid up for you, my beloved.*

She is basically saying, "Darling, let's go to a bed and breakfast." Remember, with everything God wants us to know spiritually, He gives us something we can see physically. He uses the imagery of the garden and the vineyard over and over. Solomon is now drinking the very best wine from the fruit of the vine. They are taking the sweetest and best fruit from this garden they have together.

Every husband is called to be a gardener.

I know a little about gardening. I plant a garden every spring and have done so for most of my adult life. Now, admittedly, it gets smaller every year. I'm down to a few tomato plants, a hill or two of melons, and maybe some zucchini, but I still enjoy it.

Gardening gives me my farmer fix that is somewhere in my DNA. My wife used to ask me why I worked so hard on it when I could just buy the very same veggies at the grocery store or farmer's market. The simple answer is I get fulfillment from something I personally planted. I enjoy eating from the "sweat of my brow." We no longer live in an agricultural society, so the image of marriage being likened to a garden might be less clear in its teaching than it was at one time. From tilling, preparing and fertilizing the soil, to planting and watering the seed, and weeding daily, gardens require a lot of work to thrive. It's not hard to understand the parallels Solomon is making to marriage.

Throughout Solomon's Song, we see the man repeatedly leading the way. He is the lead gardener. In this egalitarian society, we want everybody to be the same, but equality is not sameness. Even in this age of feminism, most women still want to be married to a strong man who is a leader. That is not the same as being married to a boss. Husbands and wives are equals (1 Peter 3:7). Wives don't need a boss; they need a leader. As the husband goes, so goes the marriage. As the father goes, often so goes the family.

Every man is called to be a gardener and to know how to love and nurture his wife so she can be as fruitful and beautiful as

God made her. Such biblical masculinity is embedded in every man who ever lived. In Genesis, God put the first man, Adam, in a garden and charged him in Genesis 2:15 to *tend it* and *keep it*. In other words, God was telling Adam to work it and go to war for it. To *keep it* was to defend it, and to *tend it* was to nurture it.

God was charging Adam ahead of time because He knew the garden would soon be under attack by Adam's enemy. Satan would soon make war on the first family to destroy them and steal the garden from them. God was telling Adam to protect their house. Remember, men have a garden called marriage and a vineyard—our wives. The same enemy that successfully made war on the first family in Genesis 3 is still doing all the same things today. In the very same way God put Adam in a garden and said, "I want you to tend it and guard it," we are to do the same.

In Genesis chapter 3, God knew there was going to be an invasion of sin, and Satan would try to destroy the first marriage. The serpent in Genesis 3 is the very same serpent today that wants to destroy your marriage and everything God wants to give you. It's imperative that we learn from Adam's failure and succeed where Adam didn't. God gives us the same charge He gave Adam to be the protector, defender, lover, and leader of our wives and our homes.

The passive, emasculated, modern American male is an overcorrection and overreaction to the sinful, misogynistic, male-dominated societies that have characterized human civilization since the fall of Adam. I have yet to hear a woman compliment her husband for being weak, not having a backbone, being unwilling to lead, and unable to make even the simplest decisions.

In fact, as a pastor, the number one thing I hear year after year from frustrated wives is that they wish their husband would be the spiritual leader of their family and take more initiative to pray with her.

Male passivity is the same problem the first couple had in the Garden of Eden. Satan successfully led the first couple to their destruction because Adam chose to stand idly by on the sidelines when he should have been going to war. He sat on the bench instead of getting on the battlefield. The text in Genesis 3 tells us he was there watching the deception unfold between the serpent and his wife. He chose to be a spectator rather than stepping into the moment for which he was created. Instead of leading courageously and accepting responsibility, he chose a posture of passivity, and the world is still reeling.

God gave Adam the very same responsibility He has given to every husband: to guard the garden, work it, and go to war for it. Since the beginning, Satan has been waging an all-out assault for one purpose—to destroy the family. Because of what happened in Genesis 3, Adam and Eve's family tree was forever altered and injured, and countless marriages have been destroyed.

Thousands of years later, Satan has never let up on his diabolical plot to destroy the family. Marriage and family are the first institutions God established for His creation. Families are the backbone and fabric of society. God loves families, while Satan hates them and wants to destroy them. It has never been more important for every man to reject passivity and accept responsibility—to make the decision to lead courageously, go to war for your family, and beat back the enemy. Adam was given a work to do, a woman to love, a will to obey, and a battle to fight. That purpose has never changed, even thousands of years later.

Grab your garden tiller and get to work.

If you want a garden that is beautiful and bountiful, the first thing you must do is till the ground and turn the soil. It does little good to plant seeds in soil that hasn't been prepared. It is the same in every marriage. Grace and forgiveness are what keep the soil of your marriage healthy and the soil of your heart soft and humble toward each other. If a wife has a hardened heart toward her husband, he, in turn, will harden his heart toward her. Likewise, if he hardens his heart toward her, she will respond in a similar manner. Being compassionate and quick to forgive one another is what will keep the soil of your hearts soft toward each other. Just like a natural garden that has not been tilled for years, it is extremely difficult to break that ground once it has hardened.

Remember, the key to having a great garden in marriage is the soil—the condition of your heart. Proverbs 4:23 tells us to *"Keep* [guard] *your heart with all diligence, for out of it spring the issues of life."* Guard your heart from becoming hard toward your spouse in times of hurt and pain, when it's easy to grow resentful. Resentment leads to bitterness that causes our hearts to become hardened. Practice Ephesians 4:32, which says, *"Be kind to one another, tenderhearted, forgiving one another, even as God in Christ forgave you."* If you try to sow seeds in hard soil, they will never bear fruit.

After tilling the soil, keep planting the seeds.

Once you prepare the soil, you must sow the seeds. No one expects to reap a harvest immediately. But if you sow the seeds and take care of the garden, eventually you are going to harvest its fruit. It's the law of the harvest recorded in Galatians 6:7 that says, *"...whatever a man sows, that he will also reap."* If you sow the seeds of unforgiveness, resentment, and bitterness, you will reap from the weeds of sin you've sown. If you sow the seeds of sin such as pornography and infidelity, you will get a harvest of pain and sadness. Sin always has fruit of its own, and it will destroy the sweet fruit of marriage.

To reap the sweetest fruit, sow seeds of love and kindness, and serve each other selflessly. Sow seeds of humility and put your spouse first. Sow the seeds of Philippians 2:3-4, *"Let nothing be done through selfish ambition or conceit, but in lowliness of mind let each esteem others better than himself. Let each of you look out not only for his own interests, but also for the interests of others."* This principle will revolutionize all of the relationships in your life, especially in your marriage.

Weed the garden daily.

The most difficult part of having a garden is keeping the weeds out. I have learned that it's easy to weed the garden if you do it daily. If you neglect it, you are going to be in trouble. It can be overwhelming to look at a garden you haven't weeded for a week or more and see it overgrown with weeds. Doing a little work each day saves you from a lot of work later. It's also true of marriage.

The problem for some marriages is that it has been too long since you weeded your garden, and it has become completely overgrown with weeds. Instead of seeing the fruit of your garden, you are seeing the effects of neglect. Some have neglected their marriage year after year. They have allowed the weeds to overtake the blossoms of love and tenderness that once were there.

I started planting a smaller garden a few years ago—one that I knew I could take care of. When I had a large garden and didn't have an opportunity to even look at it for two weeks, I realized it was too late when I got back to it. Weeds had overtaken my entire garden. The only thing I could do at that point was till it under and start over. If that resonates with you, I want to encourage you to tell your spouse that the two of you are going to till under all the months and years of discord and division and begin anew. Make a fresh start. It's not too late to start over.

Make the decision to weed your marriage every day, consistently nurturing it with grace, forgiveness, kindness, and thoughtfulness. Plant seeds daily by serving each other. Intentionally do things that will bless the other. You weed your garden by repenting quickly from sin. It is much easier and takes much less work to do it on the front end than on the back end.

In Song of Solomon chapter 7, we learn that if you truly want a fruitful marriage of love and harmony, you need to view it as a garden. Husband, you are the gardener and the leader of your family. It is your responsibility to keep the weeds of discord out of your garden.

Husband, you need to create a home that is a greenhouse for the garden—a building specially built for optimum growing conditions inside even when the weather is hostile toward growth on the outside. God reminds every husband of this in Psalm 128. If we create the right environment for our wives to thrive, our marriages will bear beautiful fruit.

> *Blessed is every one who fears the Lord, who walks in His ways. When you eat the labor of your hands, you shall be happy, and it shall be well with you. Your wife shall be like a fruitful vine in the very heart of your house...* (Psalm 128:1-3).

God is saying, if you will work the garden and go to war for your garden, if you will guard it and keep it, your wife is going to be a fruitful vine in the heart of your home. You are going to drink from the fruit of that vine that Solomon calls the very best wine. But this is not a "one and done." It takes time, and being consistent and not wavering is key.

What does it mean to fear the Lord? It means to live surrendered to Him. I don't know about you, but I want to be blessed. I don't want to live in mediocrity. I want to live in victory every day. Are you living in a place where you can be blessed? When you are "living in the fear of the Lord," you are obedient to God's commands. You can't expect God's abundant blessings if you are disobedient. His blessings are always conditional— He will do "that" when you first do "this." Your "this" is to be obedient.

> If you do not pursue what is holy, you will never be truly happy, and you will end up neither holy nor happy.

Psalm 128 says, *"Blessed is every one who fears the Lord…and you shall be happy."* I am guessing everyone who will read this book would like to be happy. More importantly, God wants you to be happy. The problem is that many people pursue a happy life without pursuing a holy life. If you do not pursue what is holy, you will never be truly happy, and you will end up neither holy nor happy.

In that same passage, David, the psalmist of Israel, said, *"Blessed is every one…who walks in His ways."* That is living obediently. He says, your wife will be like a fruitful vine. This very same woman in Song of Solomon chapter 7 has now become that fruitful vine. She said, *"Let us get up early to the vineyards; let us see if the vine has budded, whether the grape blossoms are open, and the pomegranates are in bloom. There I will give you my love."* She is saying that her love will be like the very best wine.

For Psalm 128 to become a reality in your life and home, husband, you must oversee quality control. Climate control is at our fingertips. My home must be a greenhouse for optimal growing conditions. At my home, I have peach trees, an apple tree, and a small vineyard of Concord grapes. Come August, those vines are full of ripe and oh-so-sweet grapes. Every fall, those vines that were once fruitful appear to die because the climate is beginning to change. Cold weather blows in, daylight begins to shorten, and it is no longer the right climate for growth.

For some husbands, your wife is no longer a fruitful vineyard. You have neglected your love, and the vine has begun to go dormant. Over the years, the climate of the relationship slowly changed from warm to cold. It is as though the garden has died. The keepers of the garden have allowed the climate to change from one that gave life to one that can only bring dormancy and death.

It is crucial for husbands to understand that to keep the garden as God intended, your home needs to be a spiritual greenhouse that ensures the right conditions for growth, regardless of what may be happening outside. It might be winter weather, but on the inside, it is always sunny and 75 degrees—perfect for growth and for its inhabitants to thrive. If my marriage is a garden and my wife is a vine, I need to ensure that the right conditions are met on the inside no matter what's going on outside.

Climate Control Essentials

What are the essentials for this climate control system?

Number one is to love her unconditionally. Husband, let me remind you that God did not wait for you to become lovable to love you. He loved you when you were not lovable.

But God demonstrates His own love toward us, in that while we were still sinners, Christ died for us (Romans 5:8).

You are a picture of Christ to your wife, and according to Ephesians 5:25, you are called to *"love your wives, just as Christ also loved the church and gave Himself for her."* You are never more like Christ than when you are loving your wife—even in those moments when she is not being lovable. Just like God's love has the power to transform you, your love for your bride has the power to transform her.

Remember, you are her mirror, and what she sees in the mirror becomes a self-fulfilling prophecy because you are the prophet and the pastor of your home. When you treat her like a treasure, even on the days when she doesn't act like a treasure, she will start to respond like the one God made her to be. When you tell her repeatedly that she is beautiful—even when she is not acting beautifully, eventually she is going to become more beautiful. Everything that Jesus is to you, you are called by God to be to her, loving her unconditionally.

It is not enough simply to say, "I love you," when she cannot feel your love. There have been many times in my marriage when I said, "Honey, I love you," and my wife responded, "I don't feel your love." She was saying, "I know you love me, but I want to feel that you love me."

Sometimes we try to love each other the way we want to be loved. We aren't speaking the same love language because God made us different. Much has been written about this, but we don't all give and receive love the same way.

It's important to understand how our spouse receives and interprets our love, and it's not always how we want to be loved. I have two principal love languages: words of affirmation and physical touch. My wife's primary love language is quality time together. I need less quality time to feel loved than she does. I need to be aware of this and adjust accordingly. Quality time for my wife does not include time together with the television on. It means time together talking.

The second factor needed to create the right climate for our wives to become fruitful vines is time together talking. Gentlemen, it is crucial that you understand this—your wife needs *rapport* talk, not merely *report* talk. Do you remember how much you used to talk to her when you were dating? You would be out talking until after midnight. Then you would call her before you even got home. That's what made her feel cherished and treasured. You were making those emotional deposits, which is why she fell in love with you.

Every day, think about the greenhouse of your marriage and the right factors needed for your wife to grow and become like a fruitful vine such as quality time together talking. When you do, you will pick the sweetest fruit of the vine, and that takes time. Life is busy, and with kids in the home, it's even busier.

You would be amazed at what giving your wife 30 minutes of your undivided attention every day will do for your relationship. Husband, if you want to be deeply bonded with your wife, you need to do the work and spend time talking with her. Every garden needs to be fertilized regularly to grow. For most wives, the best fertilizer for their souls is quality time together genuinely talking. I mean real conversation. It's one of the reasons she fell in love with you, and it's one of the reasons she'll stay in love with you.

It is well-published that women are naturally more verbal than men. I've been told that men speak about 15,000 words a day, while women speak about 30,000 words a day. Why does this matter? Sometimes when I come home at the end of the day, I am worn out. I feel like I have used 14,999 words, and I only have one left. But my wife is ready for time together talking. The easiest thing for me to do is report talk when what she needs is rapport talk.

She will ask me, "So, Phil, how was your day?" She is trying to reconnect with me emotionally at the end of a long day. But

I'm emotionally drained and will try to get away with report talk. "Well, I had my 7 a.m. breakfast appointment. Then I had my executive team meeting at 8:30. Then I met with some other staff until it was time for lunch. Then I had a lunch appointment, and after that, I worked on my sermon for a couple of hours…." That is not what my wife needs. She does not merely want to know what I did that day; she wants to know how my day was.

Here is a good habit for husbands to adhere to. At the end of the day, when you come home and see your wife, spend the first 20 minutes telling her the best thing about your day and then the worst thing about your day. Ask her about the best and worst parts of her day. Now you are starting to connect on a deeper level.

> ***Anything that does not get attention and intention will begin to atrophy.***

The nature of many gardens is neglect and a lack of intention. Talk to her intentionally, love her unconditionally, and you will foster **number three, *which is trust and security*.** When we introduce things like pornography into our lives and marriages, it's like blowing a hole the size of a freight train in the side of your greenhouse. Before you know it, your home is like a snowstorm, blowing in winter weather that is minus 125 degrees Fahrenheit.

A woman needs to know that you are a man of fidelity and integrity. She shouldn't have to wonder what you're doing when you're away for a week on a business trip or even for the evening for a guy's night out. She should never have to wonder who you are thinking about or what you are watching. If she has a sense of trust and security, there will be beauty and bounty in your relationship.

When you ask people about the foundation of relationships, most of the time they say love, but the real answer is trust. You can love people you don't trust. Even though you love them, if you don't trust them, you can't get close to them. Trust and fidelity are essential to having a garden that is healthy and full of bounty. So, husband, choose to be a man of integrity. Choose to walk in sexual fidelity and emotional integrity. When a woman feels secure relationally, she can give herself to you fully.

Number four is to *serve her sacrificially.* You are never more like Christ than when you are serving your bride. Jesus says in Mark 10:45, *"For even the Son of Man did not come to be served, but to serve, and to give His life a ransom for many."*

Jesus died to give life to His bride.

Ask yourself what you can do to serve your wife. Does she need you to do the dishes? Jesus washed the feet of His disciples. I think we can wash some dishes. Does she need you to change a dirty diaper? Jesus came to clean up our mess, and it's not too much that we would clean up our kids' messes so our wives don't have to.

Serve her sacrificially because this is what Christ did for you and me. He sacrificed everything. That simple act will establish the right atmosphere in your garden—an atmosphere of growth because it's deeply rooted. It may not happen immediately, but if you stay the course, it will happen sooner rather than later.

Psalm 128:3 is the promise: *Your wife shall be like a fruitful vine.*

The nature of a vine is to cling. Your wife will become like a vine that begins to cling when you are living out practically what God has already said about you positionally. You don't become one flesh on the day you say, "I do." Even though God says He no longer sees two of you but only one, practically speaking, this happens over the years as you establish the right climate in your marriage and guard and work the garden.

In my garden, my grape vines are so clingy you can hardly eradicate them. That is the imagery that God is using. Your wife will begin to cling to you, and the two of you will become one flesh.

True intimacy is the goal of marriage as God intended in the Garden of Eden. A husband's leadership should not feel like oppression to his wife, but rather liberation. This is why biblical submission has such a bad rap in our society. The concept has been misinterpreted, misapplied, abused, and misused.

Remember, husband, you are to be a picture of Christ to your wife, and He wants us to follow His leadership. Jesus says in John 8:36, *"Therefore if the Son makes you free, you shall be free indeed."* Our submission does not bring our oppression—it brings our liberation. Second Corinthians 3:17 tells us, *"...where the Spirit of the Lord is, there is liberty."*

If you're a husband, ask yourself whether your leadership helps to make your wife a better person. As she clings, she begins to climb, and she begins to realize that her husband has helped set her free from her anxieties and insecurities. When that happens, the fruit of the vine begins to be revealed. It is what Solomon says is the very best wine. At the end of Song of Solomon chapter 7, his wife has this to say:

> *The wine goes down smoothly for my beloved, moving gently the lips of sleepers. I am my beloved's, and his desire is toward me. Come, my beloved, let us go forth to the field; let us lodge in the villages. Let us get up early to the vineyards; let us see if the vine has budded, whether the grape blossoms are open,*

and the pomegranates are in bloom. There I will give you my love. The mandrakes give off a fragrance, and at our gates are pleasant fruits, all manner, new and old, which I have laid up for you, my beloved.

Proverbs 23:32 tells us there is a certain wine that you should not drink to excess. When one gets full of alcohol, it almost never has a positive outcome. God is not only teaching us about a different kind of wine—but a different fruit of the vine. It is your marriage and your wife. He is saying this is the best wine, and it takes time. There is a wine that is okay if it gets you a little intoxicated and carried away with each other.

I am frequently asked, "Pastor Phil, is there any hope for my marriage? Do you think my marriage will work?" I always respond the same way: "The question is not, will your marriage work, but will you work for your marriage? Just like the best gardens require a hardworking gardener, your marriage does too."

12

LOVING YOUR SECOND LIKE YOUR FIRST

When Jesus is your first love, and you love your second love (your spouse) like you love Jesus, you can have a love story that will last for eternity. As we begin this final chapter of Song of Solomon, our lovebirds have been married a very long time. We walked with them from the time they first met to their courtship and marriage. We watched their love grow into a beautiful and loving relationship. In chapter 8, they make the decision that they will die in love with each other.

We see five things that are required for such an enduring and committed love that lasts forever.

First and foremost, committed love is pleasurable.

Our society says you can't be married forever without it getting boring—however by the time Song of Solomon chapter 8 rolls around, the best is yet to come. The chapter begins with the lovers reunited at their country home, and the Shulamite is speaking to Solomon:

> *Oh, that you were like my brother, who nursed at my mother's breasts! If I should find you outside, I would kiss you; I would not be despised. I would lead you and bring you into the house*

of my mother, she who used to instruct me. I would cause you
to drink of spiced wine, of the juice of my pomegranate.

The Shulamite is no longer a young bride but an older woman. Some of the same images from the early days of their relationship are also found in the latter days. It only gets better. She begins with a narrative that seems odd in the 21st century. In their day, it was only culturally acceptable to show public displays of affection to an immediate family member. It was not culturally acceptable to show a public display of affection even to your husband or wife. Solomon's bride is saying, "We are in public, so we are going for a walk down the main street. If I could, even though everyone is watching, I would give you the biggest kiss of your life." It is worth noting that their committed love is not boring—it is better than ever.

Second, committed love is not only pleasurable but also providential:

> *Who is this coming up from the wilderness, leaning upon*
> *her beloved? I awakened you under the apple tree. There your*
> *mother brought you forth; there she who bore you brought you*
> *forth.*

In verse 5, Solomon is convinced that even from her birth, God ordained that he would one day marry her.

If you are single and want to be married, I understand why God would put that desire in you. Our lives are not nearly as random as many believe, and God providentially has a plan and purpose for your life. God loves you, and the same God who came to save you from your sin is more than capable of fulfilling the desires of your heart—just trust Him.

Third, committed love is permanent.

Verses 6 and 7 say: "*Set me as a seal upon your heart, as a seal upon your arm; for love is as strong as death, jealousy as cruel as the grave; its flames are flames of fire, a most vehement flame. Many waters cannot quench love, nor can the floods drown it. If a man would give for love all the wealth of his house, it would be utterly despised.*"

It is common to see men today with their girlfriend's name tattooed on their arm. As Solomon would say, "There is nothing new under the sun." But the irreversible and indelible mark is on his wife's heart, and their relationship is permanent. She is saying there is nothing that can destroy their love. It is more than tattooed on their arms—it is engraved on their hearts. Fire cannot burn it down. Water cannot wash it away. Their love is here to stay because it is a love of the Lord Jesus Christ.

In Proverbs 18:24, Solomon wrote prophetically, "*...there is a friend who sticks closer than a brother.*" Jesus is that Friend who says, "*I love you unconditionally, infinitely, and passionately. I am not going to walk away. I am here to stay.*" Ultimately, our love and marriage are meant to mirror our love relationship with our Savior.

Fourth, committed love is pure.

> *We have a little sister, and she has no breasts. What shall we do for our sister in the day when she is spoken for? If she is a wall, we will build upon her a battlement of silver; and if she is a door, we will enclose her with boards of cedar.*

Verses 8 and 9 are a flashback of the Shulamite's brothers before their sister reached puberty. She was just a little girl, maybe nine or ten years old. Now that she is engaged to be married, her brothers say they want her to be a wall and not a door that is easy for anyone to go in and out of and open to all.

> *I am a wall, and my breasts like towers; then I became in his eyes as one who found peace.*

The Shulamite is saying in verse 10, that her husband has free access, and all other men do not. She keeps herself completely and exclusively for her husband. This is a marriage and a love that is walking in purity and fidelity.

Fifth, committed love remembers the past.

> *Solomon had a vineyard at Baal Hamon; he leased the vineyard to keepers; everyone was to bring for its fruit a thousand silver coins.*

We are finally going to find out how they met. In verse 11, they are reminiscing about how God brought them together in Solomon's vineyard at Baal Hamon. He leased the vineyards to keepers, and everyone was to bring 1,000 silver coins for its fruit. The woman he would marry was a hired hand in one of his vineyards. One day when he went to check on them, he saw a beautiful young lady that he had never seen before.

She says in verse 12: *"My own vineyard is before me. You, oh Solomon, may have a thousand, and those who tend its fruit two hundred."*

You might say love is very much alive. They are very much in love in the present, even as they remember their past.

This may be the most important key of all: Part of how you connect your life to the present is never forgetting the past and how God brought you together.

CONCLUSION

In her book *Revealing Divorce,* Christy Bieber writes that the divorce rate in America is 43 percent for first marriages, 60 percent for second marriages, and a whopping 73 percent for third marriages. These dismal statistics do nothing to reveal the number of unhappy and unhealthy marriages where people would get a divorce if they felt they could afford a divorce. The good news in the middle of the bad news is that this doesn't have to be you!

My grandfather and grandmother, LT and Cora Hopper, were married 63 years before being separated by death. My father and mother, Van and Judy Hopper, were married 55 years before being separated by death. You probably know others who had lifelong marriages and whose love endured over the course of a lifetime together. What is the secret to marriages that last? Jesus gives us a clue as to what we should do in Revelation 2:4-5:

> *Nevertheless I have this against you, that you have left your first love. Remember therefore from where you have fallen; repent and do the first works, or else I will come to you quickly and remove your lampstand from its place—unless you repent.*

These words were spoken by Jesus and penned by the apostle John to the church at Ephesus—a great church that received much commendation from the Lord. However, they *"left their first love."*

Jesus still wanted to be their first and only love. As the bride of Christ, it wasn't enough that they were still going through the motions of serving Him. He wanted their heart. While these words were spoken by Jesus as a Bridegroom to a different kind of bride, I'm convinced they can be applied to all bridegrooms and all brides.

Notice that Jesus didn't say they had "lost" their first love. It says they "left" their first love. Love is more than a feeling. It's more than an emotion—it's also a choice. Love is not something you lose but something you leave.

That means that if you've fallen out of love, you can choose to fall in love again. And for clarity, just because you've fallen out of a feeling doesn't mean you've fallen out of love. True love that endures is so much more than a feeling.

> True love that endures is so much more than a feeling.

Throughout the course of a 50 or 60-year marriage, a couple will probably fall in and out of that lovin' feeling many times. A marriage will ebb and flow; feelings will come and go. But a marriage doesn't have to be lost, even when it feels like love has been lost. They never lost it. They unwittingly left it, which means it can be found. You can fall in love again, even if you don't like each other right now. This is what I learned in 2006, in year 14 of my marriage.

Jesus says to do three things:

1. Remember. Remember the early days and the things that made you fall in love. Remember the happy memories you made together when your love was new. I remember how excited I was to see Christa when she surprised me with a visit during my freshman football camp. I remember talking to her on the phone for hours and selling my blood plasma every month to pay for my long-distance phone bill. I remember being in my apartment at the University of Kansas when I heard a knock on the door. Christa had driven three hours to see me. She didn't call to tell me she was coming because she wanted to surprise me. It was a wonderful surprise, and we spent about three hours together that evening before she drove back to Springfield, Missouri, to be in class the next day. I remember how it made me feel loved.

I also made an unexpected visit to see her that following spring. She was surprised and happy to see me when I arrived in Springfield on a Friday night. We didn't have much money, but we scraped together enough to buy a pizza. We didn't need an expensive date. We were together, and that's all that mattered. We cherished the time we spent together and treasured each other.

We spent lots of time talking together. This is how two people fall in love.

Jesus says we should "remember" because you stay in love or fall back in love by doing the same things that made you fall in love. After the wedding, people often stop doing the things that made them fall in love. That's why Jesus says that after you remember, you need to...

2. Repent. Repent of anything you've allowed to come between you and the one you promised to love. Repent of the sin that you've brought into your marriage.

Romans 6:23 says, *"The wages of sin is death...."* Sin always brings death to marriages.

Remember, divorce itself is not always a sin, but it's always sin that causes divorce. Pornography is a marriage killer. Adultery and infidelity are marriage killers. But sometimes, the sin that destroys marriages is far more subtle. It's not death by a single blow but rather thousands of smaller blows that take a toll over time. Repent of any neglect, lack of attention, or lack of intention.

We might begin neglecting each other's needs emotionally or physically or take for granted the one we promised to cherish above all others. We begin treating the marriage God calls sacred as trivial. We quit going on dates and talking about meaningful things together.

Sometimes it's not on purpose—life just got busy. The kids came. Work got in the way. Or worse yet, a pattern of abuse may have set into your marriage. It's easy to use our words in a way that brings death instead of life. James 3:6 says, *"And the tongue is a fire, a world of iniquity."*

Like fire, the words that come off your tongue can either warm your marriage with love and joy or completely burn it down. You didn't fall in love by speaking hurtful words that berated or disrespected each other.

Take an inventory of any sinful patterns in your marriage that threaten to destroy it, and repent! Repent simply means to turn around. Admit it's wrong and choose to do right. First, confess your sins to Jesus and ask for His forgiveness. Then, confess your sins to your spouse and seek forgiveness. The next thing Jesus says to do is…

3. Return. Jesus says, *"Do the first works."* In other words, go back and do the things you did in the early days when your love was first born. If you will do what Jesus says, your love can be reborn. I told you about the pivotal year for Christa and me in 2006. In year 14 of our marriage, our love was reborn. We remembered, repented, and returned.

Fourteen years earlier, when we had been married less than a year, we went on our first vacation together to Eureka Springs, Arkansas. We found a bed and breakfast with cute, quaint, rock cottages. My young bride loved the way they looked. They screamed romance.

I walked inside to inquire about the price and found out the cottages were $85 a night. We were young and didn't have a lot of money. My jaw dropped, and I turned around and walked back to the car. I told Christa, "There is no way we're spending $85 a night!" I found a campsite for $10 a night where we set up our tent, blew up the air mattress, and went to bed. It was hardly a romantic vacation for a newlywed couple. A dog barked all night, a thunderstorm blew in, our tent blew down the hill, and we spent the night in my pickup truck. That was the summer of 1992.

In the summer of 2006, I surprised Christa with a trip back to Eureka Springs, where I made reservations at the same rock cottages where she wanted to stay all those years before. The price had more than doubled, but I didn't care. We fell back in love because we "remembered, repented, and returned." And all these years later, we are still going strong.

Remember, repent, return.

James 4:14 tells us, *"For what is your life? It is even a vapor that appears for a little time and then vanishes away."* It seems like only yesterday when I stood in front of the band room during my junior year of high school, watching the new girl with pretty green eyes walk down the hall. It seems like only yesterday I was a senior in high school going on a date for the first time with the new girl with the pretty green eyes. It seems like only yesterday I opened the door of my dorm room during my freshmen football camp to see the girl with the pretty green eyes standing there. What a surprise! It seems like only yesterday when I stood at the altar in front of my pastor to marry the new girl with the pretty green eyes. And it seems like only yesterday when the new girl with the pretty green eyes made me a daddy for the very first time.

But none of that happened yesterday. It has now been many years ago. If you're not old enough to have experienced that life is truly a "vapor," take it from someone who is. I was young once, and so was the new girl with the pretty green eyes.

I don't even know when it happened. We were young...and then we weren't. But those early years, as good as they were, were not the "good ol' days." After more than 30 years of marriage, *these* are the "good ol' days." These are the best days. And by God's grace, the best days are still ahead for Christa and me. I pray by God's grace we will live to see 50 or even 60 years of marriage together. But take it from me. Don't blink. It goes faster than you think. Choose to make Jesus the center of your every decision.

When Jesus is the center of your life, the best days are always ahead!

I pray by God's grace that is the kind of marriage He will give you. But *your decisions, not your intentions, will define your destination.* The life you live when you're old is the summation of the decisions you made along the way.

I'm so glad I decided to turn to my wife in the darkness of that night in 2006. I'm so glad I chose to "remember, repent, and return," so that I could grow old with the wife of my youth. When you humble your heart before God and let Jesus be the center of your life, the best days are always ahead, no matter how young or old you are.

May God bless you and keep you, and may He shine His face upon you and give you peace.

ABOUT THE AUTHOR

Phil Hopper has been the lead pastor of Abundant Life Church in Lee's Summit, Missouri, since 2000. He has witnessed God do extraordinary things in the life of the church, which started with 100 people and has grown to multiple campuses across Kansas City and church houses across North America.

Before becoming a pastor, he was a police officer and sergeant with the Kansas City Police Department, where he served as a SWAT team member. It was through this experience that God uniquely prepared him for the ministry.

Phil lives in the Lee's Summit area with his wife, Christa.

In the Right Hands, This Book Will Change Lives!

Most of the people who need this message will not be looking for this book. To change their lives, you need to **put a copy of this book in their hands.**

Our ministry is constantly seeking methods to find the people who need this anointed message to change their lives. **Will you help us reach these people?**

Extend this ministry by sowing 3 books, 5 books, 10 books, or more today, and become a life changer! Your generosity will be part of catalyzing the Great Awakening that many have been prophesying and praying for.